Harvard Business Review

ON

TALENT MANAGEMENT

THE HARVARD BUSINESS REVIEW PAPERBACK SERIES

The series is designed to bring today's managers and professionals the fundamental information they need to stay competitive in a fast-moving world. From the preeminent thinkers whose work has defined an entire field to the rising stars who will redefine the way we think about business, here are the leading minds and landmark ideas that have established the *Harvard Business Review* as required reading for ambitious businesspeople in organizations around the globe.

Other books in the series:

Harvard Business Review Interviews with CEOs

Harvard Business Review on Advances in Strategy

Harvard Business Review on Appraising Employee Performance

Harvard Business Review on Becoming a High Performance Manager

Harvard Business Review on Brand Management

Harvard Business Review on Breakthrough Leadership

Harvard Business Review on Breakthrough Thinking

Harvard Business Review on Bringing Your Whole Self to Work

Harvard Business Review on Building Personal and Organizational Resilience

Harvard Business Review on Business and the Environment

Harvard Business Review on the Business Value of IT

Harvard Business Review on Change

Harvard Business Review on Compensation

Harvard Business Review on Corporate Ethics

Harvard Business Review on Corporate Governance

Harvard Business Review on Corporate Responsibility

Harvard Business Review on Corporate Strategy

Harvard Business Review on Crisis Management

Harvard Business Review on Culture and Change

Harvard Business Review

ON

TALENT MANAGEMENT

A HARVARD BUSINESS REVIEW PAPERBACK

The *Harvard Business Review* articles in this collection are available as
individual reprints. Discounts apply to quantity purchases. For information and ordering, please contact Customer Service, Harvard Business
School Publishing, Boston, MA 02163. Telephone: (617) 783-7500 or
(800) 988-0886, 8 A.M. to 6 P.M. Eastern Time, Monday through Friday.
Fax: (617) 783-7555, 24 hours a day. E-mail: custserv@hbsp.harvard.edu.

Library of Congress Cataloging-in-Publication Data
Harvard business review on talent management.
    p.   cm. — (A Harvard business review paperback)
    Includes index.
    ISBN-978-1-4221-2294-5
    1. Personnel management.   2. Employees—Recruiting.
3. Manpower planning.   I. Harvard business review.
HF5549.H34425   2008
658.3—dc22   2007046191

Contents

Harvard Business Review

ON

TALENT MANAGEMENT

What It Means to Work Here

TAMARA J. ERICKSON AND LYNDA GRATTON

Executive Summary

WHAT DISTINGUISHES A COMPANY that has deeply engaged and committed employees from another one that doesn't? It's not a certain compensation scheme or talent-management practice. Instead, it's the ability to express to current and potential employees what makes the organization unique. Companies with highly engaged employees articulate their values and attributes through "signature experiences"—visible, distinctive elements of the work environment that send powerful messages about the organization's aspirations and about the skills, stamina, and commitment employees will need in order to succeed there.

Whole Foods Market, for example, uses a team-based hiring and orientation process to convey to new employees the company's emphasis on collaboration and decentralization. At JetBlue, the reservation system is

1

run by agents from their homes, a signature experience that boosts employees' satisfaction and productivity.

Companies that successfully create and communicate signature experiences understand that not all workers want the same things. Indeed, employee preferences are an important but often overlooked factor in the war for talent. Firms that have engendered productive and engaged workforces address those preferences by following some general principles: They target potential employees as methodically as they target potential customers; they shape their signature experiences to address business needs; they identify and preserve their histories; they share stories—not just slogans—about life in the firm; they create processes consistent with their signature experiences; and they understand that they shouldn't try to be all things to all people.

The best strategy for coming out ahead in the war for talent is not to scoop up everyone in sight but to attract the *right* people—those who are intrigued and excited by the environment the company offers and who will reward it with their loyalty.

It's the HR equivalent of keeping up with the Joneses: In their quest to find and retain top talent, businesses often try to match competitors' offers, ensuring that their compensation schemes, health care benefits, training programs, and other talent-management practices are in line with the rest of the industry's. While this strategy may be useful for bringing job candidates to the door, it's not necessarily the most effective way to usher the right people across the threshold—great employees who will be enthusiastic about their work and fiercely loyal to the organization and its mission.

Nor does marching in lockstep with industry standards prompt companies to consider what's unique about their histories and values or potential employees' attitudes about work. Certainly, reasonable pay and a breadth of health care options matter to prospective hires, as do the tasks they'll have to perform. But people also choose jobs—and, more important, become engaged with their work—on the basis of how well their preferences and aspirations mesh with those of the organization.

Imagine yours is one of three job offers a talented candidate is mulling over. She hears a little about the orientation program at each firm. At your company, the first three months are probationary: As a new hire, the candidate would work closely with an assigned team, and when 90 days are up, the team members would vote on whether she stays or goes. Management won't have the final say. At the second company, the candidate would work on a series of fast-paced, creative projects during her first three months, under the close scrutiny of senior management. At the end of that period, she'd be expected to find a project that matched her skills. In the third company, the new hire would undergo intensive training during the first three months, learning the organization's well-defined ways of doing business; after that, she would apprentice for an extended period with one of the firm's strongest performers.

None of these orientation experiences is inherently better than the others; the prospect will pick the company whose entry program most closely reflects her own values and preferences. If she loves risk and can put up with ambiguity, she might relish the challenges and the pace of the second company but would probably be miserable with the constraints of the third. If she enjoys collaborative work, she might gravitate toward your company.

These examples underscore the importance of employee preferences in the war for talent. Unfortunately, they are often overlooked. What truly makes good companies great is their ability to attract and retain the right people—employees who are excited by what they're doing and the environment they're operating in. Such people are more likely to be deeply engaged in their work and less likely to chase after slightly better salaries or benefits. They will find ways to satisfy their own preferences and aspirations while meeting the organization's need to come up with creative and productive solutions to business problems. Their commitment becomes contagious, infecting customers and prospective employees. Indeed, engaged employees are the antithesis of hired guns rotating in and out of critical roles—they're productive for the long term.

You won't find and keep such individuals simply by aping other companies' best practices or talent-management moves, however. You need to be able to tell new and prospective hires what it's like to work at your company, to articulate the values and attributes that make working at your firm unique. You need to provide a "signature experience" that tells the right story about your company. In the process, you'll empower the people who share your values and enthusiasm for work to self-select into your firm, thereby creating the foundation for highly productive employee-employer relationships.

Bringing Distinctiveness to Life

A signature experience is a visible, distinctive element of an organization's overall employee experience. In and of itself, it creates value for the firm, but it also serves as a powerful and constant symbol of the organization's culture and values. The experience is created by a bundle of everyday routines, or signature processes, which are tricky for competitors to imitate precisely because they have evolved in-house and reflect the company's heritage and the leadership team's ethos.

The concept of signature experiences grew out of organizational research we've conducted during the past five years. Initially, we looked closely at companies with highly engaged employees (as measured by workplace surveys and other tools) and set out to compile a checklist of the common practices these businesses used to foster enthusiastic, committed, mission-aware employees at all levels. Surprisingly, their approaches to talent management varied greatly. For instance, some firms paid well above the mean while others paid below it. Some boasted highly flexible, self-scheduling work groups; others featured more structured, "all hands on deck" environments. The companies' underlying philosophies about the employer-employee relationship also varied, from paternalistic to hands-off.

The more we looked, the more we realized that the variation in practices was not just noise in the system; it was, in fact, a critical element of the companies' ability to achieve high levels of employee engagement. (See the insert "Elements of Engagement" at the end of this article.) These organizations excel at expressing what makes them unique. They know what they are, and it's not all things to all people. They understand their current and future employees as clearly as most companies understand their current and future customers. They recognize that individuals work for different reasons and accomplish tasks in different ways. And they demonstrate what they are vividly, with stories of actual practices and events, not through slogans on the wall or laminated values cards on every desk. As a consequence, these companies hire people who easily and enthusiastically fit in, and thereby cultivate a more committed workforce. To understand how these companies attract, engage, and retain the right kind of talent, let's take a closer look at the three signature orientation experiences we described earlier.

WHOLE FOODS MARKET

The first signature experience—team-based hiring— is similar to the orientation experience at Austin, Texas–based Whole Foods Market. Potential hires are informed that each department in each store (meat, vegetables, bakery, and so on) comprises a small, decentralized entrepreneurial team whose members have complete control over who joins the group. After a four-week trial period, team members vote on whether a new hire stays or goes; the trainee needs two-thirds of the team's support in order to join the staff permanently. This signature experience is in line with Whole Foods' profit-sharing program. Thirteen times a year, the company calculates the performance of each team. Members of the teams that do well receive up to $2 per hour extra in their paychecks. That bonus pay is explicitly linked to group rather than individual performance, so team members choose their trainees carefully—they want workers, not buddies. This entry into the company undoubtedly weeds out lone wolves and conveys a strong message about the firm's core values of collaboration and decentralization. This signature experience seems to be working: Whole Foods has appeared on *Fortune*'s list of the 100 Best Companies to Work For nine years in a row.

TRILOGY SOFTWARE

The second orientation experience described earlier—trial under fire—is patterned after the signature experience at Trilogy Software, a rapidly growing software and services provider also based in Austin, Texas. New employees go through an exhausting three-month immersion process, a sort of organizational boot camp, in which top management, including the CEO, oversees their every step. In the first month, new recruits participate in fast-paced creative projects, in teams of about 20, under the mentorship of more-experienced colleagues called section leaders. In the second month, the project teams are shuffled and split into smaller "breakthrough teams" charged with inventing product or service ideas, creating business models, building prototypes, and developing marketing plans—all in hyperaccelerated fashion. In the third month, the recruits have to demonstrate their capacity for personal initiative. Some continue working on their breakthrough teams; others find sponsors elsewhere in the company and work on their projects. Upon completion of the program, candidates undergo rigorous evaluation and receive detailed feedback on their performance from colleagues, section leaders, and senior management. The new hires are sent to different parts of the organization, but the bonds they develop during this extreme orientation period remain strong throughout their careers.

Trilogy's signature orientation experience serves as the company's primary R&D engine: Recruits' projects have produced more than $25 million direct revenues and have formed the basis for more than $100 million in new business. The experience also serves as a proving ground for Trilogy's next generation of leaders: the

mentors and coaches who guide the members of the
breakthrough teams as well as the new hires themselves.
Most important, Trilogy's orientation experience provides a compelling illustration of life in the firm. A candidate who prefers a clear-cut, well-defined work environment will almost certainly decline after hearing the
details of the immersion process. But a candidate who
likes intense challenges and can tolerate some ambiguity
early on will probably jump right in.

THE CONTAINER STORE

The third orientation experience—extensive training
and indoctrination in a proven approach—is from the
Container Store, a Dallas-based retailer of storage solutions ranging from the basic (Tupperware) to the sophis-
ticated (customized shelving systems). Some of its products are quite expensive—a single custom-designed
closet system, for instance, may cost several thousand
dollars—so the floor staff's ability to meet customers'
expectations can have huge financial implications.
Because the company depends on employees to be capable of suggesting storage options that will match a customer's requirements, its induction process consists of
immediate and intense training. All new hires in the
stores, distribution centers, and headquarters (full-time
and seasonal employees) go through Foundation Week—
five days dedicated to absorbing information about the
Container Store's products, processes, and values, plus
extracurricular HR paperwork and reading. New employees assume regular work schedules only after having
completed the five full days of training—and even then
they usually apprentice for a while with some of the company's star performers. The employee education doesn't

stop there: In their first year at the Container Store, all staffers receive at least 235 hours of formal training, compared with an average of about seven hours in the retail industry overall. Employees spend time in different functions and units to gain a broader perspective and to learn about the company's strategic challenges.

The Container Store's signature experience sends the right messages about employee fit and long-term opportunities: More than 40% of new employees are recommended by friends who work for the company. Employee surveys reveal that, on average, 97% of them agree with the statement, "People care about each other here." And employee turnover is less than 30%, significantly lower than the industry average. Obviously, some job applicants will be impressed with the clarity and rigor of the Container Store's commitment to training; others won't. But a hiring manager's description of this intense orientation experience certainly sends a clear signal to a potential employee about what it takes to succeed at the company.

By defining and communicating their core values and distinctive attributes in unique and memorable ways, Whole Foods Market, Trilogy Software, and the Container Store empower potential hires to make well-informed employment choices. These companies likewise are increasing the probability that they're bringing aboard highly engaged and highly motivated workers.

Finding Your Signature

Companies that successfully create and communicate signature experiences understand that different types of people will excel at different companies, and that not all workers want the same things. In a series of studies conducted jointly with researchers Ken Dychtwald and Bob Morison, Tamara Erickson categorized workers into six segments on the basis of why and how they like to work. Some care deeply about the social connections and friendships formed in the workplace, for instance. Others just want to make as much money with as much flexibility and as little commitment as possible. Some have an appetite for risk. Others crave the steadiness of a well-structured, long-term climb up the career ladder. (See the exhibit, "A Job by Any Other Name.")

The firms we've studied that have engendered highly productive, highly engaged workforces acknowledge and address these differences more effectively than their competitors. Specifically, they follow some general principles for creating, supporting, and preserving their unique employee experiences:

Target a segment of potential employees. Most executives can tell you which consumers will buy their products or services. Few have the same insight into which job candidates will buy into the organization's culture and adapt to its workflow. Companies that target potential employees as methodically as they do potential customers can gain a sustainable market advantage. That's been the case at JetBlue. Since its launch in 1999, the airline has defied many common industry practices, including the traditional approach to flight reservations. When most airlines were using standard call centers, JetBlue devised a system based entirely out of employees' homes. This has become one of the airline's signature experiences and part of its organizational lore, attracting a strong and productive base of employees who find flexible schedules more valuable than above-average compensation.

According to founder and CEO David Neeleman, it was more than cost savings that prompted the company to create this signature experience. Like the flight crew, the reservations agents are the face of JetBlue, responsible for ensuring high levels of customer satisfaction that will translate into increased revenues. The company couldn't afford to pay the agents huge salaries, however, so senior management decided to appeal to them in a different way—by letting them work from their homes. "We train them, send them home, and they are happy," Neeleman says.

JetBlue tries to accommodate call center agents' varied scheduling requirements—some may work only 20 hours a week, for instance, or may need to swap shifts at the last minute—but the airline balances those preferences against its business objectives. Employees have unlimited shift-trading privileges, which they can negotiate using an online community board. This self-scheduling process keeps employees motivated and satisfied, which means they're more likely to provide better customer care. For its part, JetBlue has enjoyed a 30% boost in agent productivity, a 38% increase in customer-service levels, and a 50% decrease in management workload per agent, compared with industry norms.

Bright Horizons, a leading provider of employer-sponsored child care, has crafted a signature experience that also begins with the reconceptualization of a critical organizational role—that of the classroom teachers in its centers. These individuals are never referred to by common terms such as "child care worker" or "babysitter." Instead, Bright Horizons hires "early childhood educators" for its classrooms, thereby attracting people who see themselves as long-term professionals in a field full of temp workers. This important shift sets the stage for an

A Job by Any Other Name

As many societies become increasingly affluent, more and more people have the luxury of allowing work to fill a variety of roles in their lives. Studies conducted by Tamara Erickson and researchers Ken Dychtwald and Bob Morison suggest that work plays six general roles, which correspond to six types of employees, based on psychodemographic characteristics. Each worker segment cares deeply about several aspects of the employee-employer relationship and little about the others.

Employee Type	The Role of Work	What Appeals and Engages
Expressive Legacy	Work is about creating something with lasting value.	Autonomy Entrepreneurial opportunities Creative opportunities Stimulating tasks that enable continual learning and growth
Secure Progress	Work is about improving one's lot in life and finding a predictable path.	Fair, predictable rewards Concrete compensation, solid benefits and retirement package Stability Structure and routine Career training
Individual Expertise and Team Success	Work is about being a valuable part of a winning team.	Collaboration Fun Stability and structure Opportunity to gain competence Opportunity to leverage personal strengths

Employee Type	The Role of Work	What Appeals and Engages
Risk and Reward	Work is one of multiple opportunities to live a life filled with change and excitement.	Opportunity to improve personal finances Flexibility Opportunity to choose tasks and positions from a long menu of options Open-ended tasks and approaches to getting work done
Flexible Support	Work is a source of livelihood but not yet (or not currently) a priority.	Flexibility Well-defined vacation and family benefits Well-defined work routines—the ability to plug in and out of tasks and assignments with ease Virtual, asynchronous tasks and assignments Fun
Low Obligation and Easy Income	Work is a source of immediate economic gain.	Jobs that are relatively easy to come by Well-defined work routines Lucrative compensation and benefits packages Stability and security Recognition

Source: A statistical survey of the U.S. workforce conducted jointly by the Concours Institute and Age Wave, a research and communications company, and funded by 24 major corporations.

employee experience in line with the firm's mission statement, which, among other things, pledges to "nurture each child's unique qualities and potential" and to "create a work environment that encourages professionalism." Reinforcing this signature experience are the company's team-based approach to hiring; a welcome program that makes it clear to new hires (and their families) that they have joined an organization that is serious about excellence and professionalism; and strong skills-based training and promotion opportunities. In an industry known for high turnover—the average is about 50%—Bright Horizon's turnover runs from 20% to 22%.

Address specific business needs. Some companies' signature experiences stem from critical business needs. For instance, several years ago Lord John Browne, the CEO of BP, was faced with the daunting task of bringing together five oil companies BP had recently acquired. The challenge was to create a culture of learning across the company's 120 business units; without such integration, none of the anticipated cost-benefit synergies would materialize. At the time, many of the business unit heads were adept at competing, but few were adept at collaborating. To address this gap, Browne and his colleagues developed a signature experience called "peer assist." The business unit heads are assigned to peer groups representing as many as 13 units, and the members are required to exchange ideas and information about what is and is not working in their businesses. (To encourage knowledge sharing, much of each business unit leader's bonus pay depends on the performance of the whole peer group.) Employees are learning from one another. Thanks in part to these cross-platform groups,

BP has met its financial targets and talent-management criteria. The beauty of this signature experience is that it clearly demonstrates Browne's basic operational philosophy: Peers working together will be the foundation of BP's success. Managers who can't buy into the signature experience won't waste their time or the organization's.

Identify and preserve your history. The seed of a signature experience already exists in many companies. Their challenge is to find it, extend or shape it to the needs of today's business, and protect it. Consider Royal Bank of Scotland, which can credit its rise from a small national bank to one of the largest financial institutions in the world to a work environment that values action and speed. Those who do best in the bank deliver high-quality results quickly and under intense pressure— which is why prospects need to hear about RBS's historic signature experience.

In the eighteenth century, when the financial institution was founded, banking was a gentleman's pursuit. The day's business was usually completed by lunchtime so that businessmen could get on to more important matters in the afternoon—fishing, hunting, and the like. That schedule was made possible by the morning meeting. Now, of course, banking is a 24-hour business, and there's much less time for afternoon jaunts through the Scottish hills. But the morning meeting lives on. Successive RBS CEOs have adopted this practice and made it their own. The current executive team meets with the chief executive, Sir Fred Goodwin, every morning between 8 and 9 to talk about the previous day's events, go over that day's agenda, and plan for the future. The sessions force employees to think about speed to market;

RBS talks about completing projects within 30, 60, or 90 days—there is no mention of weeks or months. The morning meetings reinforce the collective accountability of the senior team.

RBS knows that early morning meetings and short-term, fast-paced projects won't appeal to everyone. So its signature experience sends an explicit message to potential hires: There are plenty of jobs out there for those who need a caffeine jolt and a few minutes with the *Times* before making a decision—just not at RBS.

Another firm with a signature experience rooted in its history is W.L. Gore & Associates, a private firm headquartered in Delaware. The company's best-known product, Gore-Tex, is used in clothing worn by adventurers the world over. W.L. Gore attributes its steady growth to an employee experience built around the so-called "lattice" system of management—no hierarchies, no predetermined channels of communication, and no defined jobs locking associates (they're never called employees) into particular tasks. This approach, which founder Bill Gore introduced more than 40 years ago, has been protected and reinforced ever since. Associates have sponsors, not bosses. They don't have jobs; they make voluntary promises to meet general expectations within functional areas—running a particular machine, for instance, or crunching numbers. For their part, sponsors commit to helping new associates find "quick wins"— projects that put the recruits on a fast track for success while acclimatizing them to the organization.

W.L. Gore's general processes uphold this signature experience. For instance, associates are compensated on the basis of the quantity, quality, and financial outcomes of their work. Performance is reviewed twice each year,

and peers and sponsors get to weigh in on their colleagues' work. They share their feedback with a compensation committee—there are about 15 such committees
within the company, one for each functional area of the
business—that then ranks people who handle a particular function from the highest contributor to the lowest.
(The associate's rank is determined by contributions to
the success of the business, not just personal achievements.) Using guidelines based on external salary data,
the company pays the associates at the top of the list
more than those at the bottom. The objective is to be
internally fair and externally competitive.

Employees who want clear definition in their work
would probably hate W.L. Gore's emphasis on personal
ownership and commitment; those who are comfortable
in a high-reward but somewhat uncertain environment
would be likely to thrive.

Share your stories.   One of the legends any MBA stu-
dent is likely to hear is that of Goldman Sachs's signature
recruitment experience. Successive cohorts of B-school
students worldwide pass along the tale of the MBA stu-
dent who went through 60 interviews before being hired.
That story isn't an urban myth. The selection process is
truly an endurance test, requiring enormous resources.
In a given year, about 5,000 applicants speak to ten members of the firm, and the top 2,500 speak to more than 30.
Each year, Goldman Sachs invests more than 100,000
man-hours in conversations with prospective employees.

The seemingly endless interviews are not designed to
ferret out candidates' intellectual prowess or previous
work experiences—that's what the GMAT scores and
application forms are for. The process is a reflection of the

company's deep commitment to internal collaboration and networking and serves as a preview of life in the firm. At Goldman Sachs, there is no room for individual stars. Prospective candidates who hear the stories and enjoy meeting partners in the myriad interview sessions are exactly those, the firm believes, who will be capable of building networks and strong collaborative relationships.

Employees at Starbucks have their own tales to pass on. When recruiting baristas, the company looks for people with outgoing personalities and strong social skills. To convey these attributes and prompt customer-savvy individuals to self-select into the firm, Starbucks tells all prospective hires about its mandatory in-store immersion process. Every new Starbucks employee—even at the corporate level—goes through a 24-hour paid training module called First Impressions. The standardized curriculum focuses on learning about coffee and creating a positive customer experience. This is followed by in-store training—employees spend time making beverages, talking to customers, and learning the business on the floor. Employees at all levels say this hands-on experience is essential preparation for any role within the company. And they swap stories about candidates who ditched the process early on, just because they didn't want to spend weeks working in the stores. Indeed, the satisfied lot who stuck with it and poured lattes for a while tell these tales with great pride.

Strive for consistency. A signature experience must be buttressed by processes that send consistent messages to employees. Our research shows that one of the most common causes of low engagement in organizations is employees' perception that some elements of the work experience aren't exactly as they were advertised.

How many times have we all heard people, six months into a job, say, "It's just not what I expected or wanted."

Several years ago, a large industrial company asked us to help redesign its orientation process, which executives at the firm felt was turning people off and driving them away. When we took a close look, we concluded that the orientation process wasn't the problem; it accurately reflected the highly structured, tightly managed nature of the organization. The problem was occurring much earlier, during recruitment, when the company promised prospective employees a flexible work environment full of excitement and innovation. This company was not a bad place to work, but it was doing a poor job of targeting and attracting people who would thrive there. It needed to change either the pitch it used with job candidates or the experience of working at the firm.

Whole Foods backs up its team-based induction process with compensation practices, employee rewards and recognition, and promotion criteria that are also strongly team based. All elements of the overall employee experience are aligned. Likewise, Goldman Sachs's commitment to cooperative networks and its "one firm" mentality are reinforced in multiple ways, including through its promotion practices. Attention is given not only to an individual's commercial acumen but also to the extent to which he or she is a culture carrier for the company. Representatives across the company, not just within specific divisions or product lines, participate in the evaluation and selection of partners.

Have the courage of your convictions. Companies— even very large ones—don't need to be all things to all people. In fact, they shouldn't try to be. No matter the content of your signature experience, you can attract people who are suited to your organization's culture and interested in furthering its goals. Conversely, you must be willing to accept that your employment proposition won't appeal to everyone. Exxon Mobil, for instance, readily acknowledges that its highly structured environment isn't for everyone, and a number of employees choose to leave early in their tenures. The company's demands are exacting; employees are expected to follow clear communication protocols and strict security regulations—as you might expect in an industry in which safety is a high priority. Interestingly, however, attrition among employees who make it past the five-year mark is almost nil, and the level of engagement among them is very high. Perhaps there's a more effective way for the company to communicate the structured nature of its work experience to prospective hires, but Exxon Mobil's signature experience is strong enough and cohesive enough to retain those who are likely to be engaged and productive in the firm for the long term.

The company's executives calmly recognize their plight. "The suit was too tight," they say, as they describe those who departed early on. That statement serves as a polite but powerful reminder that Exxon Mobil's employee experience is unlikely to flex on the basis of one individual's preferences and that opting out is an acceptable path. Management understands that the company's signature experience won't necessarily map to every stage of the employee life cycle. And management carefully and sensitively protects the processes that contribute to this secure, structured experience. For example, the company recently considered switching from a defined benefits plan to a defined contribution plan, which the majority of companies today favor for their employees. In the end, it concluded that the security the defined benefits plan provides is more in sync with the values of the employees the company hopes to retain.

People will become long-term, deeply engaged employees of your company if their work experience is what they expect it to be and if your firm's values and attributes match theirs. You do a disservice to your organization—and to prospective employees—if you try to be all things to all people. The best strategy for coming out ahead in the war for talent isn't to scoop up everyone in sight, unless you want to deal with the fallout: high turnover, high recruitment and training costs, and disengaged, unproductive employees. Instead, you need to convince the right people—those who are intrigued and excited by the work environment you can realistically offer and who will reward you with their loyalty—to choose you.

Elements of Engagement

TO FOSTER DEEPLY COMMITTED EMPLOYEES, you need the following:

- A comprehensive understanding of the types of people who will be productive in your organization over the long term. What kinds of skills should they have? What should be their attitudes toward work?

- A well-defined, well-communicated signature experience that conveys for potential hires and reinforces for employees the attributes and values of the organization.

- A coherent employee experience—none of your company's environmental elements misrepresents what it's really like to work there.

Originally published in March 2007
Reprint R0703G

A Players or A Positions?

The Strategic Logic of
Workforce Management

MARK A. HUSELID, RICHARD W. BEATTY,
AND BRIAN E. BECKER

Executive Summary

COMPANIES SIMPLY CAN'T AFFORD to have "A players" in all positions. Rather, businesses need to adopt a portfolio approach to workforce management, systematically identifying their strategically important A positions, supporting B positions, and surplus C positions, then focusing disproportionate resources on making sure A players hold A positions.

This is not as obvious as it may seem, because the three types of positions do not reflect corporate hierarchy, pay scales, or the level of difficulty in filling them. A positions are those that directly further company strategy and, less obviously, exhibit wide variation in the quality of the work done by the people who occupy them. Why variability? Because raising the average performance of individuals in these critical roles will pay huge dividends in corporate value. If a company like Nordstrom, for example, whose strategy depends on personalized service, were to improve the performance of its frontline sales associates, it could reap huge revenue benefits.

B positions are those that support A positions or maintain company value. Inattention to them could represent a significant downside risk. (Think how damaging it would be to an airline, for example, if the quality of its pilots were to drop.) Yet investing in them to the same degree as A positions is ill-advised because B positions don't offer an upside potential. (Pilots are already highly trained, so channeling resources into improving their performance would probably not create much competitive advantage.) And C positions? Companies should consider outsourcing them—or eliminating them.

We all know that effective business strategy requires differentiating a firm's products and services in ways that create value for customers. Accomplishing this requires a differentiated workforce strategy, as well.

A GREAT WORKFORCE is made up of great people. What could be more intuitively obvious? Is it any wonder, then, that so many companies have devoted so much energy in recent years to identifying, developing, and retaining what have come to be known as "A players"? Firms like GE, IBM, and Microsoft all have well-developed systems for managing and motivating their high-performance and high-potential employees—and for getting rid of their mediocre ones. Management thinkers have widely endorsed this approach: Larry Bossidy, in the best-selling book *Execution,* for example, calls this sort of differentiation among employees "the mother's milk of building a performance culture."

But focusing exclusively on A players puts, well, the horse before the cart. High performers aren't going to add much value to an organization if they're smoothly and rapidly pulling carts that aren't going to market. They're going to be effective only when they're harnessed to the right cart—that is, engaged in work that's essential to company strategy. This, too, may seem obvious. But it's surprising how few companies systematically identify their strategically important A *positions*—and *then* focus on the A players who should fill them. Even fewer companies manage their A positions in such a way that the A players are able to deliver the A performance needed in these crucial roles.

While conventional wisdom might argue that the firms with the most talent win, we believe that, given the financial and managerial resources needed to attract, select, develop, and retain high performers, companies simply can't afford to have A players in all positions. Rather, we believe that the firms with the *right* talent win. Businesses need to adopt a portfolio approach to workforce management, placing the very best employees in strategic positions, good performers in support positions, and eliminating nonperforming employees and jobs that don't add value.

We offer here a method for doing just that, drawing on the experience of several companies that are successfully adopting this approach to workforce management, some of which we have worked with in our research or as consultants. One thing to keep in mind: Effective management of your A positions requires intelligent management of your B and C positions, as well.

Identifying Your A Positions

People traditionally have assessed the relative value of jobs in an organization in one of two ways. Human resource professionals typically focus on the level of skill, effort, and responsibility a job entails, together with working conditions. From this point of view, the most important positions are those held by the most highly skilled, hardest-working employees, exercising the most responsibility and operating in the most challenging environments.

Economists, by contrast, generally believe that people's wages reflect the value they create for the company and the relative scarcity of their skills in the labor market. Thus, the most important jobs are those held by the most highly paid employees. The trouble with both of these approaches is that they merely identify which jobs the company is currently treating as most important, not the ones that actually are. To do that, one must not work backward from organization charts or compensation systems but forward from strategy.

That's why we believe the two defining characteristics of an A position are first, as you might expect, its disproportionate importance to a company's ability to execute some part of its strategy and second—and this is not nearly as obvious—the wide variability in the quality of the work displayed among the employees in the position.

Plainly, then, to determine a position's strategic significance, you must be clear about your company's strategy: Do you compete on the basis of price? On quality? Through mass customization? Then you need to identify your strategic capabilities—the technologies, information, and skills required to create the intended competitive advantage. Wal-Mart's low-cost strategy, for instance, requires state-of-the-art logistics, information systems, and a relentless managerial focus on efficiency and cost reduction. Finally, you must ask: What jobs are critical to employing those capabilities in the execution of the strategy?

Such positions are as variable as the strategies they promote. Consider the retailers Nordstrom and Costco. Both rely on customer satisfaction to drive growth and shareholder value, but what different forms that satisfaction takes: At Nordstrom it involves personalized service and advice, whereas at Costco low prices and product availability are key. So the jobs critical to creating strategic advantage at the two companies will be different. Frontline sales associates are vital to Nordstrom but hardly to be found at Costco, where purchasing managers are absolutely central to success.

The point is, there are no inherently strategic positions. Furthermore, they're relatively rare—less than 20% of the workforce—and are likely to be scattered around the organization. They could include the biochemist in R&D or the field sales representative in marketing.

So far, our argument is straightforward. But why would variability in the performance of the people currently in a job be so important? Because, as in other portfolios, variation in job performance represents upside potential—raising the average performance of individuals in these critical roles will pay huge dividends in corporate value. Furthermore, if that variance exists across companies, it may also be a source of competitive advantage for a particular firm, making the position strategically important.

Sales positions, fundamental to the success of many a company's strategy, are a good case in point: A salesperson whose performance is in the 85th percentile of a company's sales staff frequently generates five to ten times the revenue of someone in the 50th percentile. But we're not just talking about greater or lesser value creation—we're also talking about the potential for value creation versus value destruction. The Gallup organization, for instance, surveyed 45,000 customers of a company known for customer service to evaluate its 4,600 customer service representatives. The reps' performance ranged widely: The top quartile of workers had a positive effect on 61% of the customers they talked to, the second quartile had a positive effect on only 40%, the third quartile had a positive effect on just 27%—and the bottom quartile actually had, as a group, a negative effect on customers. These people—at the not insignificant cost to the company of roughly $40 million a year (assuming average total compensation of $35,000 per person)— were collectively destroying value by alienating customers and, presumably, driving many of them away.

Although the $40 million in wasted resources is jaw-dropping, the real significance of this situation is the huge difference that replacing or improving the performance of the subpar reps would make. If managers focused disproportionately on this position, whether through intensive training or more careful screening of the people hired for it, company performance would improve tremendously.

The strategic job that doesn't display a great deal of variability in performance is relatively rare, even for those considered entry-level. That's because performance in these jobs involves more than proficiency in carrying out a task. Consider the job of cashier. The generic mechanics aren't difficult. But if the position is part of a retail strategy emphasizing the customers' buying experience, the job will certainly involve more than scanning products and collecting money with a friendly smile. Cashiers might, for example, be required to take a look at what a customer is buying and then suggest other products that the person might want to consider on a return visit. In such cases, there is likely to be a wide range in people's performance.

Some jobs may exhibit high levels of variability (the sales staff on the floor at a big-box store like Costco, for example) but have little strategic impact (because, as we have noted, Costco's strategy does not depend on sales staff to ensure customer satisfaction). Neither dramatically improving the overall level of performance in these jobs nor narrowing the variance would present an opportunity for improving competitive advantage.

Alternatively, some jobs may be potentially important strategically but currently represent little opportunity for competitive advantage since everyone's performance is already at a high level. That may either be because of the standardized nature of the job or because a company or industry has, through training or careful hiring, reduced the variability and increased the mean performance of workers to a point where further investment isn't merited. A pilot, for example, is a key contributor to most airlines' strategic goal of safety, but owing to regular training throughout pilots' careers and government regulations, most pilots perform well. Although there definitely is a strategic downside if the performance of some pilots were to fall into the unsafe category, improving pilot performance in the area of safety is unlikely and, even if marginal gains are possible, unlikely to provide an opportunity for competitive advantage.

So a job must meet the dual criteria of strategic impact and performance variability if it is to qualify as an A position. From these two defining characteristics flow a number of others—for example, a position's potential to substantially increase revenue or reduce costs—that mark an A position and distinguish it from B and C positions. B positions are those that are either indirectly strategic through their support of A positions or are potentially strategic but currently exhibit little performance variability and therefore offer little opportunity for competitive advantage. Although B positions are unlikely to create value, they are often important in maintaining it. C positions are those that play no role in furthering a company's strategy, have little effect on the creation or maintenance of value—and may, in fact, not be needed at all. (For a comparison of some attributes of these three types of positions, see the exhibit "Which Jobs Make the Most Difference?")

It's important to emphasize that A positions have nothing to do with a firm's hierarchy—which is the criterion executive teams so often use to identify their organizations' critical and opportunity-rich roles. As natural as it may be for you, as a senior executive, to view your own job as among a select group of vital positions in the company, resist this temptation. As we saw in the case of the cashier, A positions can be found throughout an organization and may be relatively simple jobs that nonetheless need to be performed creatively and in ways that fit and further a company's unique strategy.

A big pharmaceutical firm, for instance, trying to pinpoint the jobs that have a high impact on the company's success, identifies several A positions. Because its ability to test the safety and efficacy of its products is a required strategic capability, the head of clinical trials, as well as a number of positions in the regulatory affairs office, are deemed critical. But some top jobs in the company hierarchy, including the director of manufacturing and the corporate treasurer, are not. Although people in these jobs are highly compensated, make important decisions, and play key roles in maintaining the company's value, they don't *create* value through the firm's business model. Consequently, the company chooses not to make the substantial investments (in, say, succession planning) in these positions that it does for more strategic jobs.

A positions also aren't defined by how hard they are to fill, even though many managers mistakenly equate workforce scarcity with workforce value. A tough job to fill may not have that high potential to increase a firm's value. At a high-tech manufacturing company, for example, a quality assurance manager plays a crucial role in making certain that the products meet customers' expectations. The job requires skills that may be difficult to find. But, like the airline pilots, the position's impact on company success is asymmetrical. The downside may indeed be substantial: Quality that falls below Six Sigma levels will certainly destroy value for the company. But the upside is limited: A manager able to achieve a Nine Sigma defect rate won't add much value because the difference between Six Sigma and Nine Sigma won't be great enough to translate into any major value creation opportunity (although the difference between Two- and Three-Sigma defect rates may well be). Thus, while such a position could be hard to fill, it doesn't fit the definition of an A position.

Managing Your A Positions

Having identified your A positions, you'll need to manage them—both individually and as part of a portfolio of A, B, and C positions—so that they and the people in them in fact further your organization's strategic objectives.

Which Jobs Make the Most Difference?

An A position is defined primarily by its impact on strategy and by the range in the performance level of the people in the position. From these two characteristics flow a number of other attributes that distinguish A positions from B and C jobs.

	A Position: Strategic	B Position: Support	C Position: Surplus
Defining characteristics	Has a direct strategic impact AND Exhibits high performance variability among those in the position, representing upside potential	Has an indirect strategic impact by supporting strategic positions and minimizes downside risk by providing a foundation for strategic efforts OR Has a potential strategic impact, but exhibits little performance variability among those in the position	May be required for the firm to function but has little strategic impact
Scope of authority	Autonomous decision making	Specific processes or procedures typically must be followed	Little discretion in work
Primary determinant of compensation	Performance	Job level	Market price

Effect on value creation	Creates value by substantially enhancing revenue or reducing costs	Supports value-creating positions	Has little positive economic impact
Consequences of mistakes	May be very costly, but missed revenue opportunities are a greater loss to the firm	May be very costly and can destroy value	Not necessarily costly
Consequences of hiring wrong person	Significant expense in terms of lost training investment and revenue opportunities	Fairly easily remedied through hiring of replacement	Easily remedied through hiring of replacement

A first and crucial step is to explain to your workforce clearly and explicitly the reasons that different jobs and people need to be treated differently. Pharmaceutical company GlaxoSmithKline is identifying those positions, at both the corporate and business-unit levels, that are critical to the company's success in a rapidly changing competitive environment. As part of that initiative, the company developed a statement of its workforce philosophy and management guidelines. One of these explicitly addresses "workforce differentiation" and reads, in part: "It is essential that we have key talent in critical positions and that the careers of these individuals are managed centrally."

But communication is just the beginning. A positions also require a disproportionate level of investment. The performance of people in these roles needs to be evaluated in detail, these individuals must be actively developed, and they need to be generously compensated. Also, a pipeline must be created to ensure that their successors are among the best people available. IBM is a company making aggressive investments on each of these four fronts.

In recent years, IBM has worked to develop what it calls an "on-demand workforce," made up of people who can quickly put together or become part of a package of hardware, software, and consulting services that will meet the specific needs of an individual customer. As part of this effort, IBM has sought to attract and retain certain individuals with what it terms the "hot skills" customers want in such bundled offerings.

In the past year or so, the company has also focused on identifying its A positions. The roster of such positions clearly will change as IBM's business does. But some, such as the country general manager, are likely to retain their disproportionate value. Other strategic roles include mid-level manager positions, dubbed "deal makers," responsible for the central strategic task of pulling together, from both inside and outside the company, the diverse set of products, software, and expertise that a particular client will find attractive.

EVALUATION

Because of their importance, IBM's key positions are filled with top-notch people: Obviously, putting A players in these A positions helps to ensure A performance. But IBM goes further, taking steps to hold its A players to high standards through an explicit process—determining the factors that differentiate high and low performance in each position and then measuring people against those criteria. The company last year developed a series of ten leadership attributes—such as the abilities to form partnerships with clients and to take strategic risks—each of which is measured on a four-point scale delineated with clear behavioral benchmarks. Individuals assess themselves on these attributes and are also assessed by others, using 360-degree feedback.

DEVELOPMENT

Such detailed evaluation isn't very valuable unless it's backed up by a robust professional development system. Drawing on the strengths and weaknesses revealed in their evaluations and with the help of tools available on the company's intranet, people in IBM's A positions are required to put together a development program for themselves in each of the ten leadership areas.

This is only one of numerous development opportunities offered to people in A positions. In fact, more than $450 million of the $750 million that IBM spends annually on employee development is targeted at either fostering hot skills (both today's and those expected to be tomorrow's) or the development of people in key positions. A senior-level executive devotes all of his time to programs designed to develop the executive capabilities of people in these jobs.

COMPENSATION

IBM supports this disproportionate investment in development with an even more disproportionate compensation system. Traditionally at IBM, even employees with low performance ratings had received regular salary increases and bonuses. Today, annual salary increases go to only about half the workforce, and the best-performing employees get raises roughly three times as high as those received by the simply strong performers.

SUCCESSION

Perhaps most important, IBM has worked to formalize succession planning and to build bench strength for each of its key positions, in part by investing heavily in feeder jobs for those roles. People in these feeder positions are regularly assessed to determine if they are "ready now," "one job away," or "two jobs away" from promotion into the strategically important roles. "Pass-through" jobs, in which people can develop needed skills, are identified and filled with candidates for the key strategic positions. For example, the position of regional sales manager is an important pass-through job on the way to becoming a country general manager. In this way, IBM ensures that its A people will in fact be ready to fill its top positions.

Managing Your Portfolio of Positions

Intelligently managing your A positions can't be done in isolation. You also need strategies for managing your B and C positions and an understanding of how all three strategies work together. We find it ironic that managers who embrace a portfolio approach in other areas of the business can be slow to apply this type of thinking to their workforce. All too frequently, for example, companies invest in their best and worst employees in equal measure. The unhappy result is often the departure of A players, discouraged by their treatment, and the retention of C players.

To say that you need to disproportionately invest in your A positions and players doesn't mean that you ignore the rest of your workforce. B positions are important either as support for A positions (as IBM's feeder positions are) or because of any potentially large downside implications of their roles (as with the airline pilots). Put another way, although you aren't likely to win with your B positions, you can certainly lose with them.

As for those nonstrategic C positions, you may conclude after careful analysis that, just as you need to weed out C players over time, you may need to weed out your C positions, by outsourcing or even eliminating the work.

Roche is one firm that is placing more emphasis on the strategic value of positions themselves. Over the past few years, the pharmaceutical company has been looking at different positions to determine which are necessary for maintaining competitive advantage. Regardless of how well a person performs in a role, if that position is no longer of strategic value, the job is eliminated. For example, Roche looked at the strategic value provided by data services in a recent project and as a result decided which positions need to be added, which needed to change (or be moved)—and which, such as data center services (DCS) engineer, needed to be eliminated. In a similar manner, another pharmaceutical firm, Wyeth Consumer Healthcare, following a strategic decision to focus on large customers, eliminated what had been a strategic position for the company—middle-market account manager—as well as staff that supported the people in this position.

The ultimate aim is to manage your portfolio of positions so that the right people are in the right jobs, paying particular attention to your A positions. First, using performance criteria developed for determining who your A, B, and C players are, calculate the percentage of each currently in A positions. Then act quickly to get C players out of A positions, replace them with A players, and work to help B players in A positions become A players. GlaxoSmithKline currently is engaged in an initiative to push both line managers and HR staff to ensure that only top-tier employees (as determined by their performance evaluations) are in the company's identified key positions.

Making Tough Choices

Despite the obvious importance of developing high-performing employees and supporting the jobs that contribute most to company success, firms that routinely make difficult decisions about R&D, advertising, and manufacturing strategies rarely show the same discipline when it comes to their most valuable asset: the workforce. In fact, in our long experience, we've found that firms with the most highly differentiated R&D, product, and marketing strategies often have the most generic or undifferentiated workforce strategies. When a manager at one of these companies does make a tough choice in this area, the decision often relates to the costs rather than the value of the workforce. (The insert "Are We Differentiating Enough?" at the end of this article can help you determine whether you are making the distinctions likely to create workforce value.)

It would be nice to live in a world where we didn't have to make hard decisions about the workforce, but we don't. Strategy is about making choices, and correctly assessing employees and roles are two of the most important. For us, the essence of the issue is the distinction between equality and equity. Over the years, HR practices have evolved in a way that increasingly favors equal treatment of most employees within a given job. But today's competitive environment requires a shift from treating everyone the same to treating everyone according to his or her contribution.

We understand that this approach may not be for everyone, that increasing distinctions between employees and among jobs runs counter to some companies' cultures. There is, however, a psychological as well as a strategic benefit to an approach that initially focuses on A positions: Managers who are uncomfortable with the harsh A and C *player* distinction—especially those in HR, many of whom got into the business because they care about people—may find the idea of first differentiating between A and C *positions* more palatable. But shying away from making the more personal distinctions is also unwise. We all know that effective business strategy requires differentiating a firm's products and services in ways that create value for customers. Accomplishing this requires a differentiated workforce strategy, as well.

Are We Differentiating Enough?

MANAGERS WHO KNOW that differentiated strategies are the key to competitive success all too often fail to differentiate in strategies for their most important asset—their workforce. This checklist can help you determine if you are differentiating enough in the treatment of your company's positions and people. If you check off any of these, you have work to do.

Positions

- Position descriptions are based on history, not strategic value.

- Most positions are paid at about the market midpoint.

- Recruitment and retention for all positions involve the same effort and budget.

- The same selection process is used for all positions.

- Little developmental rotation occurs.

- Few C positions are eliminated or outsourced.

Players

- Performance evaluation forms are completed rarely or only at salary review.

- There is little candor in performance reviews.

- Many or most employees are rated the same.

- Forced distribution of ratings is used.

- Those receiving the middle rating are labeled "proficient" or "successful" and receive regular pay raises despite being viewed as average or marginal.

- Both very tough and very lenient raters operate without consequences.

- Poor performers stay yet don't improve.

- Top management is not rigorously evaluated.

Originally published in December 2005
Reprint R0512G

Growing Talent as If Your Business Depended on It

JEFFREY M. COHN, RAKESH KHURANA, AND LAURA REEVES

Executive Summary

TRADITIONALLY, corporate boards have left leadership planning and development very much up to their CEOs and human resources departments—primarily because they don't perceive that a lack of leadership development in their companies poses the same kind of threat that accounting blunders or missed earnings do.

That's a shortsighted view, the authors argue. Companies whose boards and senior executives fail to prioritize succession planning and leadership development end up experiencing a steady attrition in talent and becoming extremely vulnerable when they have to cope with inevitable upheavals—integrating an acquired company with a different operating style and culture, for instance, or reexamining basic operating assumptions when a competitor with a leaner cost structure emerges. Firms that haven't focused on their systems for building their bench strength will probably make wrong decisions in these situations.

In this article, the authors explain what makes a successful leadership development program, based on their research over the past few years with companies in a range of industries. They describe how several forward-thinking companies (Tyson Foods, Starbucks, and Mellon Financial, in particular) are implementing smart, integrated, talent development initiatives.

A leadership development program should not comprise stand-alone, ad hoc activities coordinated by the human resources department, the authors say. A company's leadership development processes should align with strategic priorities. From the board of directors on down, senior executives should be deeply involved in finding and growing talent, and line managers should be evaluated and promoted expressly for their contributions to the organizationwide effort. HR should be allowed to create development tools and facilitate their use, but the business units should take responsibility for development activities, and the board should ultimately oversee the whole system.

IN THE THIRTEENTH CENTURY, it took the College of Cardinals almost three years to anoint a successor to Pope Clement IV. To break the stalemate, one of history's most bitter organizational deadlocks, church officials began limiting the food and drink they provided the voting cardinals, eventually giving them just bread and water. Fortunately, today's cardinals don't seem to need such harsh incentives: It took them less than a week to choose Benedict XVI.

When it comes to succession planning (and, by extension, leadership development) in the business world, corporate boards could do with a similar sense of urgency—though we wouldn't necessarily advocate starving them into it. Traditionally, boards have left these tasks very much up to their CEOs and human resources departments. There's a simple reason why directors pay so little attention to these activities: They don't perceive that a lack of leadership development in a company poses the same kind of threat that accounting blunders or missed earnings do.

That's a shortsighted view. Companies whose boards and senior executives fail to prioritize succession planning and leadership development end up either experiencing a steady attrition in talent or retaining people with outdated skills. Such firms become extremely vulnerable when they have to cope with inevitable organizational upheavals—integrating an acquired company with a different operating style and culture, for instance, or reexamining basic operating assumptions when a competitor with a leaner cost structure emerges. In situations like these, businesses need to have the right people in the right roles to survive. But if leadership development has not been a primary focus for CEOs, senior management teams, and boards, their organizations will be more likely to make wrong decisions. Firms may be forced to promote untested, possibly unqualified, junior managers. Or they might have to look outside for executives, who could then find it difficult to adjust to their new companies and cultures.

Some companies, however, not only have recognized the importance of including succession planning and leadership development on the board's agenda but have also taken steps to ensure that those items get on the docket. Over the past three years, we have undertaken extensive fieldwork with many of these companies, conducting multiple interviews and analyzing their varied approaches to successful leadership planning and development. We have found that the best of their programs all share some common attributes. They are not stand-alone, ad hoc activities coordinated by the human resources department; their development initiatives are embedded in the very fabric of the business. From the board of directors on down, senior executives are deeply involved, and line managers are evaluated and promoted expressly for their contributions to the organizationwide effort.

By engaging managers and the board in this way, a company can align its leadership development processes with its strategic priorities. The company can also build a clear and attractive identity; its employees perceive that leadership development processes are what they are declared to be. Such coherence, identity, and authenticity, in turn, make it easier for the company to attract the future leaders it needs.

In the following pages, we'll describe what some of the companies we've been observing are doing to create strong, effective succession-planning and leadership development programs. First, let's take a closer look at where many companies go wrong when they set out to grow great managers.

Every Which Way

Tyson Foods, a family-controlled company based in Springdale, Arkansas, provides a good example of where companies can fall short in leadership development. Every time CEO John Tyson, grandson of the company

founder with the same name, picked up a journal, news-
paper, or business magazine, he saw yet another story of
how iconic companies like General Electric set the standard in churning out future leaders, and he was frustrated in his ambition to leave a similar legacy.

It was a big ambition. Despite Tyson's size after its
merger with IBP in 2001—the company's market cap was
around $25 billion, putting it well into the *Fortune* 100—
it had, in its 70 years, invested very little in leadership
development. And the organization had no ingrained
systems, tools, or processes to ensure a steady supply of
qualified talent. When he took the reins in 2000, Tyson
had made it his goal to change all that, and the company,
over the next two years, experimented with several
leadership development initiatives.

These experiments all followed a similar course. Typically, Tyson or a member of his senior management team
would read an article or hear about an interesting initiative at another company, such as a mentoring program.
Then he or one of his colleagues would chat with Ken
Kimbro, the senior vice president of corporate HR, about
the possibility of implementing a comparable program at
Tyson (the Tyson Mentor Program, for instance). A few
weeks later, a Tyson version of the initiative would be
discussed in internal focus groups, and pilots would be
developed.

One time, John Tyson was invited by the CEO of a
prominent company to see how that organization monitored its emerging leaders' progress. When he returned
to the offices, he cleared out an entire conference room
and plastered on its walls pictures of Tyson's rising-star
managers, with descriptions of their job experiences,
educational backgrounds, strengths and weaknesses, and
development paths. Another time, Tyson personally

approved a budget to send the company's high-potential managers to leadership retreats on a remote Rio Grande ranch. The managers worked to solve actual business challenges facing the company, reflected on their personal leadership styles, and broadened their spheres of influence by meeting other high-potentials within the company. For its part, Tyson's HR group found it hard to keep up with the rush of programs.

Despite John Tyson's efforts and the popularity of many of his initiatives, the company's talent pipeline was still not producing enough quality leaders, and by the summer of 2002, the CEO realized that his ad hoc approach to leadership development was not working. He formed a senior executive task force to look into the problem. The team included himself, his direct reports, and a small group of external succession-planning experts, who were there to ensure objectivity and high standards and to help facilitate buy in.

The task force members took nothing for granted. They sat down with a blank sheet of paper and mapped out their ideal leadership development system for Tyson. The blueprint they came up with integrated succession planning and leadership development, made sure that promising leaders would be well versed in all aspects of the company's business, and put the accountability for succession planning and leadership development squarely on the shoulders of John Tyson's direct reports. "Leaders at all levels were either in or out," Tyson recalled. They couldn't waffle about contributing their time and effort to the new talent development system; they couldn't "protect" talent, hoard resources, or declare themselves immune from succession planning, he said.

An Integrated Approach

Succession planning was the critical starting point for
Tyson's new program—as it was for all the leading-edge
companies we observed. Succession planning should
drive leadership development at a company; that sounds
reasonable enough but is hard for many managers to
accept. That's because many people, from the CEO on
down, consider the word "succession" taboo. Planning
your exit is like scheduling your own funeral; it evokes
fears and emotions long hidden under layers of defense
mechanisms and imperceptible habits. Perversely, the
desire to avoid this issue is strongest in the most successful CEOs. Their standard operating procedure is to
always look for the next mountain to climb, not to step
down from the mountain and look for a replacement.

We recently conducted a leadership and talent management survey with 20 CEOs in large corporations, representing a variety of industries and locations. Although
all 20 executives agreed that having the right talent in
the right roles was critical for their companies' success
and that a talent management program was important
for developing effective leaders, almost half had no succession plans for VPs and above. Only one-fourth of the
CEOs had talent pipelines that extended at least three
managerial levels below them.

Meanwhile, those CEOs who are effective at building
strong leadership teams tend not to have any reservations about succession; they embrace succession planning and integrate it closely with the company's manage-
ment-training and development programs. When Orin
Smith became president and CEO of Starbucks in 2000,
for instance, he made it a top priority to plan his own

succession. He established an exit date—in 2005, at age 62—which helped him push his business agenda. Ultimately, Smith's actions focused attention on emerging leaders throughout the company.

Two years into the job, Smith knew that the internal contenders would still be too unseasoned for the CEO position by his exit date. Starbucks was under pressure to grow its leaders as fast as the business was expanding, from approximately 8,500 global retail locations to about 30,000 sites, half of them outside the United States. Because of his early commitment to succession planning, Smith knew enough about the internal CEO candidates—and decided on an outsider, Jim Donald, as a promising successor. Donald had an established record in supermarket expansion as chairman, president, and CEO of Pathmark, a 143-unit regional grocery chain. He was recruited to Starbucks specifically to become the next CEO.

Starbucks gave Donald 90 days of dedicated immersion. He worked in the stores to understand the customer experience, and he observed firsthand the operations in the coffee-roasting plants. Then Donald was made responsible for North American operations, Starbucks's largest business. Progressively, he became accountable for more pieces of the company. One of his first major tests was to develop his own succession plan and to execute against it in order to move to a larger role himself. Smith and Starbucks's board members paid close attention to Donald's ability to assess and develop a talented leader who could take over Donald's assignments and provide the right fit with the leadership team.

As Starbucks's experience shows, CEOs need to embrace succession planning to achieve their own legacies and the financial success of the organizations they leave behind. By integrating succession planning and talent development, CEOs can alert the rising stars in their companies to potential leadership opportunities well in advance; and they and their boards can more accurately assess their bench strength. When the process runs smoothly, boards have a strong sense of whether a company's incumbent leadership team will be able to execute important strategic initiatives in the future. The company also gains because of minimal disruption to the business, shareholder confidence and positive analyst ratings, and reduced costs of external hiring for senior executive positions.

The consumer products company S.C. Johnson & Son also uses an integrated approach. Its performance appraisal program identifies the rising stars in the company's hard-to-fill management and technical positions, evaluates them through 360-degree feedback, and determines potential leaders' readiness for promotions. The well-oiled program also includes processes to identify "safe positions"—crucial jobs with reinforced retention strategies and ready replacements. The tight integration of succession planning with talent development has paid off: The typical manager at S.C. Johnson has been on the job for nearly 15 years, and nine out of every ten positions are filled internally.

At Tyson, just a few years after the formation of the initial senior management task force on leadership development, all of John Tyson's direct reports are fully committed to the succession-planning process. In what they call the "talent alignment and optimization" initiative, or TAO, leaders from across the organization try to strike a balance between the supply of talent (rising stars) and the demand for talent (critical positions). Right after Tyson's strategic review process, which is held semiannually, the company's senior management team holds open and constructive discussions about the company's high-potential managers to ensure that the organization nurtures in them the skills necessary to execute current strategy while also preparing them to take on larger, more complex roles. And to make sure that rising stars are challenged and achieve long-term success at Tyson, the senior leaders work closely with HR to devise development paths that consider multiple career possibilities for high-potentials, three to five years out.

A Line and Board Responsibility

Many executives believe that leadership development is a job for the HR department. This may be the single biggest misconception they can have. As corporations have broken down work into manageable activities and then consolidated capabilities into areas of expertise, employee-related activities have typically fallen into HR's domain. The prevailing wisdom has been that if HR took care of those often intangible "soft" issues, line managers and executives would be free to focus on "hard" business issues and client interaction.

But at companies that are good at growing leaders, operating managers, not HR executives, are at the front line of planning and development. In fact, many senior executives now hold their line managers directly responsible for these activities. In this worldview, it is part of the line manager's job to recognize his subordinates' developmental needs, to help them cultivate new skills, and to provide them opportunities for professional development and personal growth. Managers must do this even if it means nudging their rising stars into new functional areas or business units. They must mentor emerging leaders, from their own and other departments, passing on important knowledge and providing helpful evaluations and feedback. The operating managers' own evaluations, development plans, and promotions, in turn, depend on how successfully they nurture their subordinates.

Line managers are held accountable not only for aiding in the development of individual star managers but also for helping senior executives and HR experts define and create a balanced leadership development system for the entire company. They must tackle questions such as "How will we balance the need to nurture future leaders with the pressures to eliminate redundant activities?" and "How should we encourage burgeoning leaders to take risks and innovate while maintaining our focus on short-term operations and profit goals?" (Firms shouldn't have to forgo their quarterly targets for the sake of developing high-potential managers.) Practical solutions to these and other challenges don't magically appear in HR conference rooms; they come from the line managers.

If line managers are held responsible for executing the talent development initiatives, the board should assume high-level ownership of the overall system. Traditionally, however, most boards have focused on CEO succession, giving short shrift to systematic leadership development. After all, there was little risk of a calamity occurring if the board *didn't* monitor the leadership pipeline. There was also little chance that the board members would be held personally accountable for the resulting weak talent pool. In A.T. Kearney's 2004 survey on the effectiveness of corporate governance, participating board directors universally acknowledged the importance of leadership development and succession planning. Yet only one in four respondents believed the board of directors was very good at these activities.

The CEOs of savvy companies realize that their boards are well placed to help them plan for new leadership to take the reins. Detached from day-to-day operations and biases, board directors can objectively look at the company's leadership development systems and bench strength. At Starbucks, for example, the board oversees a formalized succession-planning process for 2,500 positions. Its goal is to make sure the company always has the right people with the right values in the right places at the right times. As Orin Smith explains: "The values and behaviors of the individuals you choose go through the organization like a rifle shot; they can be felt at the line level within months. We can't afford to hire or promote people with the wrong values. It's a path to mediocrity."

Some boards are becoming aggressive in getting to know their companies' rising stars. Pittsburgh-based Mellon Financial, a 136-year-old financial institution, had long required the heads of its major business units to give presentations to the board. But in 2002, CEO Marty McGuinn saw potential value in having the company's rising stars make these presentations. Now, Mellon's unit managers accompany the rising stars to the board meetings. They answer questions when absolutely necessary, but the future leaders get the floor. As a result, the board can assess for itself the efficacy of the company's leadership pipeline and hear about corporate initiatives from the people who are actually "doing things." Meanwhile, the rising stars gain direct access to the board, gleaning new perspectives and wisdom as a result.

(See the insert "A Leadership Development Checklist" at the end of this article.)

A Shared Resource

No leadership development program can be effective unless it provides mechanisms for exposing future leaders to the full range of the company's operations. By introducing their rising stars to new business units, geographies, and business challenges (managing a turnaround, for instance, or launching a new product in a foreign market), companies can help these executive-track employees broaden their power bases and spheres of influence while giving them a sense of how the different parts of the organization work together to execute the overall corporate strategy.

It's a reasonable goal but hard to accomplish. Why would the supervisor of a brilliant junior manager share that talent with another unit, knowing that productivity and profitability in his own unit might suffer? And what if the rising star misinterprets the transfer to another business unit (with perhaps fewer people and less revenue) as a negative gesture and considers leaving the company?

Tyson Foods faced just such challenges. Under the company's revamped leadership development program, business unit heads were obliged to share their highest-performing managers with other business units so these rising stars could gain cross-functional experience. Initially, it was hard for the unit leaders to do so, after years of hoarding talent and building personal fiefdoms.

To encourage sharing, John Tyson holds the business unit and functional leaders personally accountable for rotating emerging leaders through different parts of the company. Cross-functional development plans—essentially, the road maps for high-potentials' assignments to Tyson's different businesses—are clearly articulated at the succession conferences described earlier. These plans are monitored by Tyson and the vice president of corporate HR. Moreover, the CEO assures unit leaders that they will receive equally qualified managers in exchange for their outgoing ones. The company's talent-assessment practices have been refined so that the right qualities and skills are being measured across all businesses and functions. That is, Tyson realized that a manager's success in one area of the business was by no means a guarantee of success in another. So the company carefully retrofitted its performance assessment tools to measure the competencies, values, and skills that would be necessary for any future positions that a manager might pursue. The results are objective, so business unit leaders are exchanging "apples for apples," not simply sending B players to other units and keeping their fingers crossed for a star in return. Tyson has also adopted formal performance-management review policies that link senior executive compensation to the movement and development of emerging leaders.

Mellon's Marty McGuinn has a similar philosophy. His strikingly simple but powerful mantra is "Connect the dots." That is, for Mellon to create a leadership development system that competitors cannot match, all its managers must map their discrete leadership development activities and processes to a coherent, company-wide system. Managers in dramatically different functions, locations, and operating units are expected to share knowledge and talent that they think would enhance the whole system. (The insert "A Crash Course," at the end of this article, describes how Mellon built its integrated leadership development system.)

Aligned, Attractive, and Authentic

As Tyson learned, an effective talent development program is more than just a portfolio of off-the-shelf components such as competency-profiling tools, 360-degree feedback, and online training. It is a carefully thought-out system that you have to develop for yourself.

As a CEO assessing a new program, the first question you need to ask yourself is whether the constituent parts of your program combine to enable the company to compete more effectively. A company that operates in a highly innovative environment, for example, needs to know whether its leadership development system actually enables it to produce better innovations more quickly than its competitors. If the system rewards individuals who produce the most predictable rather than the most innovative results, it is misaligned.

Misalignment usually occurs when companies have developed, tested, and rolled out initiatives ad hoc, without any high-level planning or a defined time horizon. The first iteration of Tyson's mentoring program, for instance, was barely linked to the company's existing leadership development activities and strategic goals. Little thought went into the matching process; rising stars weren't necessarily assigned mentors in the businesses and functions that could have helped them the most, so significant developmental opportunities were lost.

Misalignment can also occur when a company's 360-degree feedback and performance-management instruments measure (and reward) behaviors that are inconsistent with the company's values and culture. It may be counterproductive, for instance, to reward managers for their skills in acquiring new customers if the company's overall strategy is to focus on existing customers by cross selling and offering bundled products and services.

The second question you need to ask is whether your leadership development system reinforces the perceptions you want people to have about the company. We've found that there is a direct relationship between a strongly defined leadership development program at a company and the types of job candidates the company attracts, external stakeholders' perceptions of the business, and employees' understanding of the firm's values and strategies. For example, Starbucks employees, all of whom are called "partners," are attracted to the job in part because of the company's talent identity. They want to be that cheerful, smiling-to-the-music person behind the counter who helps customers start the day out right with a *venti* or a *grande*. The company's leadership development program reinforces this identity: Its hiring and promotion processes put equal weight on an employee's functional capabilities and his or her ability to fit in with the company's values and beliefs system. And to preserve the company's culture in this time of rapid growth, Starbucks has added a component to the program, called Leading from the Heart, which helps existing managers transmit Starbucks's customer-friendly (and brand-centric) ethos to new hires.

The third question you have to ask is whether your employees think the company's leadership programs are legitimate. They will take the program seriously only if they know these talent management elements will affect actual business decisions instead of just padding personnel folders. They must also believe that those individuals whom the system recruits, selects, and promotes are truly qualified for their positions and aren't just being rewarded for their political allegiances.

Companies need to address the issue of authenticity head-on. Senior executives at Mellon realized that some people might be skeptical about the company's new talent development initiatives: Many managers felt they were too busy dealing with day-to-day operations and client relations to take time off to attend the company's mentoring program. Recognizing this skepticism, HR included in the sessions case studies of mentoring relationships and how they helped to improve results on the job. (The sessions themselves are data driven and led by senior operating executives.) Specifically, the sessions demonstrate the positive correlation between the productive relationships a manager can have with his or her team members and the economic effectiveness of that group or division. Most executives find it a compelling proposition that, with help from the mentoring program, they can actively improve their employees' skills, increase people's commitment to work, boost information sharing, and create better-trained employees who are willing to accept greater responsibility.

THE COMPANIES that shared their stories and knowledge with us highlighted several critical aspects of leadership development—in particular, CEOs' awareness and acknowledgment of the importance of succession planning; boards' increased activity in system oversight; managers' refocused attention on people issues and processes; and HR's role in facilitating the entire organization's ownership of leadership development. As their experiences demonstrate, a leadership development program need not be a ragbag of training programs and benefits. Properly thought through, it can be a major part of a company's value proposition—one that competitors can't even understand, much less copy.

A Leadership Development Checklist

TO GROW GREAT LEADERS, companies should do the following:

- Launch a formal, high-level succession-planning conference for senior executives facilitated by corporate HR and outside experts; outline the leadership development process; and cascade it through the company.

- Create leadership development programs that fill holes in your company's talent portfolio to ensure a deep bench for critical positions in the firm.

- Let HR create tools and facilitate their use, but require the business units to own the leadership development activities.

- Have the board oversee all leadership development initiatives, and insist on continual communication by CEOs and other senior managers on their commitment to leadership development.

- Reshuffle rising stars throughout the company, taking care that A players are exchanged for other A players.

- Make sure that your leadership development program is aligned with your strategy, reinforces your company's brand, and has support from your employees.

A Crash Course

MOST OF THE COMPANIES we studied developed their leadership programs over time or at least were under relatively little pressure in terms of talent management. Mellon Financial, however, had to build a new system under extreme pressure to support senior management's efforts to transform the company.

By the late 1990s, the venerable organization comprised a wide range of businesses. The senior management team had articulated a business strategy that focused on high-growth opportunities and global expansion. Through the disposition of specific units, and through strategic acquisitions to build its asset management and corporate and institutional services businesses, senior management effectively transformed Mellon from a traditional commercial bank to a more focused financial services institution.

But CEO Marty McGuinn realized that the next generation of leaders would not be able to execute the new strategy without an enhanced set of competencies and a broader, more entrepreneurial mind-set, one that could include bundling products and services, cross selling to clients, and expanding into unproven global markets.

To meet this challenge, Mellon's HR department created an extensive leadership development program that was rolled out to the whole company. Mellon's senior management team was involved from the start. McGuinn and his team met frequently (in person and via e-mail) and conducted one-on-one discussions with emerging leaders at the company. Armed with these data, the executives helped Mellon's rising stars understand the competencies they would need and developed plans for them to acquire those skills.

But McGuinn and Mellon's human resources director knew that HR's tools for leadership development would not gain traction among managers if they were not owned and implemented by the business units. Mellon's managers had a reputation for being results driven and focused on achieving day-to-day goals. An HR-mandated mentoring program or 360-degree feedback assessment initiative, no matter how shiny and slick, might seem like a distraction to these people—and would ultimately be futile.

McGuinn, therefore, instituted a policy that leadership development tools would be created in formal centers of excellence consisting of three to six resident experts. The tools would then be offered to the business units through a specialized distribution network of human resources business partners (HRBP)—liaisons between the centers of excellence and the business unit heads. The HRBPs were charged with understanding the strategies of the business units and the competencies they wanted to develop and execute. The HRBPs would use that information to determine, in collaboration with the unit leaders, which leadership development tools to use. Because the units' strategies varied considerably across Mellon, McGuinn and HR granted the HRBPs wide latitude in their decisions about how, when, and why to use particular tools.

Originally published in October 2005
Reprint R0510C

Make Your Company a Talent Factory

DOUGLAS A. READY AND JAY A. CONGER

Executive Summary

DESPITE THE GREAT SUMS OF MONEY companies dedicate to talent management systems, many still struggle to fill key positions—limiting their potential for growth in the process. Virtually all the human resource executives in the authors' 2005 survey of 40 companies around the world said that their pipeline of high-potential employees was insufficient to fill strategic management roles.

The survey revealed two primary reasons for this. First, the formal procedures for identifying and developing next-generation leaders have fallen out of sync with what companies need to grow or expand into new markets. To save money, for example, some firms have eliminated positions that would expose high-potential employees to a broad range of problems, thus sacrificing future development opportunities that would far outweigh any initial savings from the job cuts. Second, HR executives often have trouble keeping top leaders' attention on talent issues, despite those leaders' vigorous assertions that obtaining and keeping the best people is a major priority. If passion for that objective doesn't start at the top and infuse the culture, say the authors, talent management can easily deteriorate into the management of bureaucratic routines.

Yet there are companies that can face the future with confidence. These firms don't just manage talent, they build talent factories. The authors describe the experiences of two such corporations—consumer products icon Procter & Gamble and financial services giant HSBC Group—that figured out how to develop and retain key employees and fill positions quickly to meet evolving business needs. Though each company approached talent management from a different direction, they both maintained a twin focus on *functionality* (rigorous talent processes that support strategic and cultural objectives) and *vitality* (management's emotional commitment, which is reflected in daily actions).

Despite all that is known about the importance of developing talent, and despite the great sums of money dedicated to systems and processes that support talent management, an astonishing number of companies still struggle to fill key positions—which puts a considerable constraint on their potential to grow. We conducted a survey of human resources executives from 40 companies around the world in 2005, and virtually all of them indicated that they had an insufficient pipeline of high-potential employees to fill strategic management roles.

The problem is that, while companies may have talent processes in place (97% of respondents said they have formal procedures for identifying and developing their next-generation leaders), those practices may have fallen out of sync with what the company needs to grow or expand into new markets. To save money, for example, some firms have eliminated the position of country manager in smaller nations. Since that role offers high-potential employees comprehensive exposure to a broad range of problems, however, the company's initial savings may well be outweighed by the loss of development opportunities.

Even if a company's practices and supporting technical systems are robust and up to date, talent management will fail without deep-seated commitment from senior executives. More than half the specialists who took part in our research had trouble keeping top leaders' attention on talent issues. Senior line executives may vigorously assert that obtaining and keeping the best people is a major priority—but then fail to act on their words. Some managers still believe they can find talented employees by paying a premium or by using the best executive recruiters, while others are distracted by competing priorities. Passion must start at the top and infuse the corporate culture; otherwise, talent management processes can easily deteriorate into bureaucratic routines.

The challenge of filling key positions has, in a sense, crept up on businesses, many of which used to view development almost as an employee benefit. Today, demographic shifts—notably, the impending retirement of baby boomers—along with changing business conditions, such as significant growth in largely unfamiliar markets, like China, have combined to produce something of a perfect storm. Leadership development has

become a much more strategic process, and faulty processes and executive inattention now carry a tangible .
cost. We've attended multiple executive committee
meetings where companies have been forced to pass on
hundreds of millions of dollars of new business because
they didn't have the talent to see their growth strategies
through to fruition. One London-based real estate
finance and development firm, for instance, was gearing
up for a major reconstruction job in Berlin—an effort
that would represent not only a €500 million boost in
revenues over two years, but also an opportunity to get
in on the ground floor of many other projects in that part
of the world. When the executive committee reviewed
the list of people who might be ready to take on such an
assignment, the CEO noticed that the same names
appeared as the only candidates for other critical efforts
under consideration. And when he asked his business
unit heads for additional prospects, he was told that
there weren't any. The firm's growth strategy hinged on
these projects, but the company had failed to groom people to lead them.

Some companies, by contrast, face the future with
confidence because they don't just manage talent, they
build what we call "talent factories." In other words, they
marry *functionality,* rigorous talent processes that support strategic and cultural objectives, and *vitality,* emotional commitment by management that is reflected in
daily actions. This allows them to develop and retain key
employees and fill positions quickly to meet evolving
business needs.

Consider, for example, how one talent factory, consumer products icon Procter & Gamble, found a leader
for a burgeoning joint venture with an entrepreneur in
Saudi Arabia. The role required someone with emerging

markets experience, who had worked in other countries and in the laundry detergent business, and who was ready and willing to relocate on short notice to Saudi Arabia. For most companies' HR departments, finding and hiring such a senior manager would entail protracted dialogue with internal and external candidates and might well end in failure. P&G, however, searched its global database of talent profiles and came up with five very strong potential candidates in just a few minutes. In the end, they found just the right fit, and the new manager was fully on board three months after the start of the search.

In this article, we look at the people processes in two talent factories: Procter & Gamble and financial services giant HSBC Group. We selected these companies because even though they approach talent management from slightly different directions, both illustrate the power of a twin focus on functionality and vitality. P&G has established a plethora of elaborate systems and processes to deploy talent; HSBC has worked mightily to incorporate talent processes into the firm's DNA. Both companies can claim a free-flowing pipeline of current and future leaders.

Functionality: Effective Execution

Functionality refers to the processes themselves, the tools and systems that allow a company to put the right people with the right skills in the right place at the right time, as P&G did in Saudi Arabia. Good design isn't just a matter of technical excellence; clearly linking processes to the company's objectives is equally important. In particular, processes should support most CEOs' top concerns: driving performance and creating an effective climate.

So, for example, after years of growth through acquisition, HSBC in 2002 shifted its strategy to focus on organic growth. The goal was to strengthen local resources in multiple geographies for the firm's increasingly global customers. Achieving this objective required an accompanying cultural shift, since HSBC had always operated as a confederation of fiercely independent, stand-alone businesses. As part of the move, the bank committed to a new brand promise: to be "the world's local bank," guaranteeing the availability of a local resource for customers, wherever they do business. Stephen K. Green, HSBC's chair, views performance and climate as inextricably linked: "If we don't create the proper climate internally and live up to our brand promise, we won't be able to achieve our strategic objective—managing for growth."

To develop local talent while maintaining global standards, HSBC centrally designed its human resources practices and policies but built in some flexibility to accommodate local variations. The firm now has companywide processes for assessment, recruiting, performance and career management, and leadership development, but local offices can adapt them (within limits) to their own resource capabilities and cultural requirements. When making assessments, for example, each office must choose at least two from a menu of tools, such as psychometric tests, individual interviews that probe people's aspirations, and 360-degree feedback. They must also use a standard rating scale and include performance data from the most recent three years. This way the company can ensure a degree of objectivity and establish a common measurement language across all the businesses and locations.

To help instill a global mind-set, HSBC created a system of talent pools that track and manage the careers of high-potentials within the firm. After those employees have been identified, they are assigned to regional or business unit talent pools, which are managed by local human resources and business unit leaders. Employees in these pools are then selected initially for new assignments within their region or line of business and, over time, are given positions that cross boundaries. They are viewed as having the potential to reach a senior management role in a region or a business. Managers of the pools then single out people to recommend for the group talent pool, which represents the most senior cadre of general managers and is administered centrally. These managers are considered to have the potential to reach the senior executive level in three to five years and top management in the longer term.

Leaders maintain talent relationship dialogues with members of each pool, in face-to-face conversations where possible, to address their development needs and concerns. In new relationships, the dialogues are time intensive and available to the employee on demand; in established relationships, the conversations tend to occur two to four times a year, as needed. The aim is to structure a set of experiences that leads to a deep knowledge of all aspects of the business as well as an understanding of the many different cultural environments in which HSBC operates.

In fact, people are told that if they want to reach the highest levels of management they must expect to work in at least two very different cultural environments. The number of people making such moves has increased exponentially over the past few years. "We have a Brazilian working with one of our affiliates in China, our insurance affiliate," Green told us. "We have an Armenian working in India in the IT function, a Turk working in New York. There are . . . hundreds and hundreds

Mapping Functionality and Vitality

The functionality and vitality of your company's talent management processes determine how well you can groom your high-potential employees to fill strategic management roles. To show how to assess these processes, we've mapped the strengths and weaknesses of a typical, though hypothetical, company. In this example, the organization is pursuing a "one company" strategy, hoping to achieve better global integration. In other words, it wants to be able to serve its customers anywhere they do business. Clearly, this requires a talent pool that can easily move across regional, functional, and unit boundaries, as well as the capacity to find and develop local talent "on the ground."

The Functionality Wheel shows that this firm is weak on sourcing, deployment, development, and rewards; better at retention, assimilation, performance management, and engagement. The firm may be able to keep its local talent happy and productive, but it struggles to place people in key positions or move them across unit or geographic borders.

Corporate vitality is manifested by the passion for talent management among four constituencies: the top team, line management, human resources, and talent itself. As the Vitality Wheel shows, this company neither champions the process nor holds other key stakeholders accountable for developing talent. Despite high commitment, all the segments in this firm are weak on accountability, and the top team is weak on engagement as well. Since a company's talent management process is only as strong as its weakest link, and vitality falls apart without mutual accountability, this company plainly has a lot of work to do.

Identifying weaknesses in functionality and vitality can help a company clarify its talent management agenda. If this organization wanted to grow in China, for instance, it could improve its sourcing by developing relationships with Chinese universities.

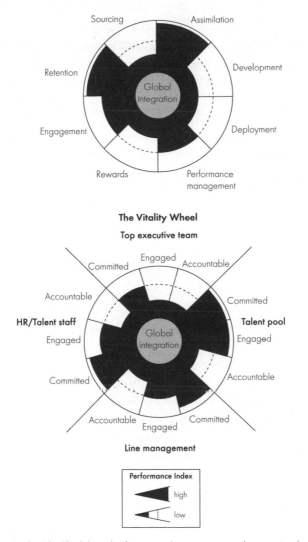

The Functionality Wheel

Sourcing · Assimilation · Development · Deployment · Performance management · Rewards · Engagement · Retention

Global integration

The Vitality Wheel

Top executive team

Committed · Engaged · Accountable

HR/Talent staff

Accountable · Engaged · Committed

Talent pool

Committed · Engaged · Accountable

Global integration

Accountable · Engaged · Committed

Line management

Performance Index

high

low

The Functionality Wheel (top) shows that this company's processes are weak on sourcing, development, deployment, and rewards; better when it comes to retention, assimilation, performance management, and engagement. The Vitality Wheel (bottom) demonstrates a high level of commitment, but engagement—the inclination to dig into the work of talent management—is low among top managers. As for accountability, the company is weak across the board.

of examples of this." Green acknowledges that this approach is expensive—it's nearly always cheaper to fill a role with someone local—but considers it a vital investment in achieving the firm's global goals.

HSBC is still tweaking the process. The bank learned, for instance, that assessing each employee on a scale of one to five was demoralizing for some people, so it modified the process to rate only people in the top two levels of some areas. Feedback for the rest is framed in terms of development needs and support, rather than "you haven't made it into a talent pool." This change takes into account early-stage career development, which entails gaining a certain amount of expertise before a person is ready to advance.

HSBC also learned that, talent pools notwithstanding, leaders of the local units still behaved as princes of their domains—they weren't connecting across units in ways that would benefit the firm overall. In short, the model of international teamwork was still more an aspiration than an operating principle. To close this gap between aspiration and reality, HSBC resolved conflicts in its reward system and took steps to build relationships on a more personal basis. So, for example, the top executive team launched what it called collective-management conferences, where employees could learn about the company's strategic objectives and operations around the world—another way to help people feel like part of an organization that extends beyond their own unit or locale. Each conference is attended by about 40 senior managers, who have been nominated by their country, functional, or customer group leader because they've demonstrated a potential for growth and because their roles have policy implications across the enterprise.

These meetings, which are held twice per year, have become a vehicle for senior people in the company to share knowledge and ideas across corporate borders and customer groups. During one conference, the general manager for Mexico told his colleagues how he managed to rebrand a recent acquisition, Grupo Financiero Bital, literally overnight. His story shed light on the value of collaborating across company boundaries. At another gathering, one of HSBC's senior executives explained how acquiring the U.S. firm Household International gave the organization much deeper capabilities in customer analytics and buying behavior. During yet another meeting, a couple of general managers explained how they built on their preexisting relationship to ease the transfer of a client from commercial banking to private banking. (In the past, the client would have been jealously guarded because his profitability would have been attributed to whichever group "owned" that customer.) After each conference, participants are asked to commit to doing one or two things differently to strengthen the firm's collaboration capabilities.

The company also established networks across countries, so that, for instance, the head of personal financial services in Hong Kong knows her counterpart in Mumbai, in Mexico City, in São Paulo, in Vancouver. These networks allow executives to participate in important virtual meetings on a regular basis for each line of business and provide them with opportunities to gather face-to-face in occasional off-site meetings.

Like HSBC, Procter & Gamble has tied its talent management processes to its strategy for growth, which means a focus on winning in the emerging markets of China, India, Latin America, the Middle East, and

Assessing Your Company's Overall Capability

To get a sense of your company's current capability, rate its strength on a scale of one to ten in the following areas. Then, write down one thing you will do to address any weakness. Your ratings will give you an idea of the areas you need to focus on.

		We're poor performers			We're OK, but nothing to cheer about			We're at or near benchmark status		
1	Do you know what skills your company needs to execute its growth objectives? What will you do to strengthen your company's capability in this area?	1	2	3	4	5	6	7	8	9	10
2	Does your company have a process for identifying, assessing, and developing its next generation of leaders in all its businesses and regions? What will you do to strengthen your company's capability in this area?	1	2	3	4	5	6	7	8	9	10
3	Do you have specific development plans for your high-potential leaders? What will you do to strengthen your company's capability in this area?	1	2	3	4	5	6	7	8	9	10
4	Are you able to deploy the right people when emerging opportunities arise, quickly and without significant disruption to other parts of your organization? What will you do to strengthen your company's capability in this area?	1	2	3	4	5	6	7	8	9	10

5 Do you have diverse and plentiful pools of talented employees who are ready, willing, and able to be deployed to new opportunities at the technical, managerial, and leadership levels of your organization?

What will you do to strengthen your company's capability in this area?

1	2	3	4	5	6	7	8	9	10

6 Do you have a diverse and plentiful pool of leaders who are capable of moving into your organization's most senior executive roles?

What will you do to strengthen your company's capability in this area?

1	2	3	4	5	6	7	8	9	10

7 Do you offer managers and executives developmental experiences specifically aimed at preparing them for the unique challenges of leading large, complex, global organizations?

What will you do to strengthen your company's capability in this area?

1	2	3	4	5	6	7	8	9	10

8 Have you, as a leader, used words and deeds to unequivocally demonstrate that you are fully committed to developing talent globally in your company?

What will you do to strengthen your company's capability in this area?

1	2	3	4	5	6	7	8	9	10

9 Would the people around you consider you actively engaged in your company's talent management initiatives?

What will you do to strengthen your company's capability in this area?

1	2	3	4	5	6	7	8	9	10

10 Do you hold your managers and leaders accountable for identifying and developing talent in their businesses, functions, and regions?

What will you do to strengthen your company's capability in this area?

1	2	3	4	5	6	7	8	9	10

Eastern Europe. The company is building what amounts to a global talent supply-chain management process, coordinated worldwide but executed locally. Hiring and promotions are the responsibility of local managers, but high-potential prospects and key stretch assignments are identified globally.

New hires tend to be local talent. Line managers in China, for instance, hire Chinese recruits. That's been the case for some time, but it used to be that key corporate roles in emerging markets went to expatriates. Now, local hires are considered growth prospects for the firm; those Chinese recruits are expected to become managers in that market. Key stretch assignments and senior positions, however, are managed globally, at the executive level. The emphasis on hiring nationals translates into a diverse pool of leadership talent for the entire corporation, especially at more senior levels: At the geography and country leader level, there are almost 300 executives who come from 36 countries, and 50% are from outside the United States. The top 40 executives come from 12 different nations, and 45% are from outside the United States. As high-potential employees advance, they move through a portfolio of senior-level jobs that are categorized according to strategic challenges, size of the business, and complexity of the market. Leadership positions for businesses or countries are earmarked for either novice or experienced general managers. A relatively small country-manager position—in Taiwan, for instance—is considered appropriate for first-time general managers. Such assignments then set up the incumbents for placement in larger countries, like Italy or Brazil, which in turn can lead to roles in clusters of countries, such as Eastern Europe or the United Kingdom.

Those last roles then become springboards or crucibles for leaders who demonstrate the potential to become senior executives.

P&G offers formal training and development programs and sometimes sends managers to external executive education programs. The lion's share of development, however, takes place on the job, with the immediate manager's support and help from mentors and teammates. A typical marketing manager, for example, will have worked with a number of different brands over a period of time. A finance manager will have gone through various assignments, ranging from financial analysis to treasury to auditing to accounting. Most managers are also placed on important multifunctional task forces or project teams from time to time. New postings and task force participation are expected to challenge employees, and they signal to managers that P&G will always offer new opportunities.

Consider the career progression of Daniela Riccardi, who has been with the company for 22 years. She started as an assistant brand manager in Italy, where she stayed for six years, advancing to brand manager. A three-year stint in Belgium as a marketing manager for cleansers and bleach followed. She then spent seven years in three Latin American countries, holding the positions of marketing director, general manager, and vice president of ever-larger divisions. From there, she became a vice president of Eastern Europe, and in 2005, she was promoted to her current position—President, Greater China. When the development of a career like Riccardi's has to be managed across business units and countries, the planning process is led collaboratively from the center by the company's CEO, A.G. Lafley; the vice chairs; the global

HR officer; and the global leaders of the various functions for their people. All this is done in partnership with the president and human resources manager at both ends of the reassignment.

People and positions are tracked in a technology-based talent management system that is sufficiently robust to accommodate all the company's more than 135,000 employees but is primarily used to track 13,000 middle- and upper-management employees. The system captures information about succession planning at the country, business category, and regional levels; includes career histories and capabilities, as well as education and community affiliations; identifies top talent and their development needs; and tracks diversity. It also makes in-house talent visible to business leaders, who no longer have to scour the company to find candidates by themselves. To keep the systems relevant, P&G has instituted a global talent review—a process by which every country, every function, and every business is assessed for its capacity to find, develop, deploy, engage, and retain skilled people, in light of specific performance objectives. For example, if the company has stated diversity hiring objectives, the review is used to audit diversity in hiring and promotions. Determinations made in these reviews are captured in a global automated talent development system and can be accessed by decision makers through their HR managers.

The company also pays close attention to the effectiveness of its recruiting processes. P&G interviewers record detailed assessments of each candidate and assign them a quantitative score, using uniform criteria. The company then regularly assesses performance against the baseline set during the interviews. P&G also evaluates the success rate of its key promotions, using quantitative and qualitative measures that cover a three-year period. Managers who improve the business and its capabilities are deemed "successful"; the company has a success rate that exceeds 90%. When derailments occur, P&G conducts a thorough "lessons learned" review.

Vitality: The Secret Weapon

If functionality is about focusing your company's talent management processes to produce certain outcomes, vitality is about the attitudes and mind-sets of the people responsible for those processes—not just in human resources but throughout the line, all the way to the top of the organization. Unlike processes, which can with some effort be copied by competitors, passion is very difficult to duplicate. Nevertheless, there are measures that companies can take to build it into their cultures. Our research shows that the vitality of a company's talent management processes is a product of three defining characteristics: *commitment, engagement,* and *accountability.* (See the exhibit "Mapping Functionality and Vitality" on page 70.)

FOSTERING COMMITMENT

P&G hires and develops people through a set of principles—such as the rules to hire at entry level and build from within—that are specifically designed to foster commitment. While people typically have long careers with the company, the average age for all employees is only 39; 38 for all managers. More than half the organization has been with P&G for less than five years. That's because the company constantly pumps in new talent and has integrated huge numbers of people through its acquisitions of Clairol, Gillette, and Wella. So, even with the relatively low attrition rate of 7.5% (including retirements), more junior managers are always coming in. P&G hires 90% of its entry-level managers straight from universities and grows their careers over time. (The relative youth of the workforce may also reflect that this approach often allows for retirement earlier than usual.) All the vice chairs and corporate officers either joined the company from universities or arrived via acquisitions. Lafley himself joined P&G right out of Harvard Business School and, over the subsequent 25-plus years, went through numerous assignments before becoming CEO.

To gain commitment early, the company also established a college intern program that offers the chance to assume real responsibility by working on important projects with the full resources of the company. Extensive intern programs can be a drain on an organization because of the time that managers must spend sponsoring, coaching, and advising the interns. P&G, however, converts former interns to full-time employees at a percentage well above that of most competitors, so the company is compensated for its investment with high-quality hires who can hit the ground running. It also assigns interns to multifunctional teams that work on business and organizational issues and present solutions to the CEO and senior management sponsors. The company often ends up implementing the suggestions those teams come up with. One of the four ideas presented in 2006, for instance, may result in accelerating the launch of a new brand; two other projects have been partially implemented.

At HSBC, commitment to talent is personified by Green, who explains, "There is nothing more important than getting this right . . . all the way from intake through the most influential senior positions." Line executives participate directly in the process, partnering with the central and regional HR functions to fill important positions.

BUILDING ENGAGEMENT

Engagement reflects the degree to which company leaders show their commitment to the details of talent management. P&G engages employees in their own career development the day they start with the company. They work with their hiring managers to plot moves that will build what the company calls "career development currency." For high-potentials, P&G identifies "destination jobs," which are attainable only if the employee continues to perform, impress, and demonstrate growth potential. The purpose is to view job assignments through a career development lens. For instance, a manager whose destination job is to become a president of one of P&G's seven regions will go through assignments in different locations to acquire international experience and work in a global business unit with responsibility for a major product category.

University recruiting is a line-led activity at P&G, and many senior managers personally lead campus teams at top universities around the world. These executives are held accountable for hiring only graduates with outstanding track records in both academic and nonacademic performance (such as summer jobs, clubs, and entrepreneurial activities). To bolster ties with these institutions, the campus team leaders also fund research, make technology gifts, participate in the classroom, and judge case study competitions.

As for HSBC, a conversation with Green makes his engagement immediately clear. Green has a remarkable knowledge of the company's day-to-day people processes and can speak at length about how the company approaches recruitment, where managers are deployed, how their careers are progressing, and what they will need to do to continue advancing. Down through the ranks, line engagement in talent management is ensured by specific policies and practices, such as the require-ment that each unit have a talent implementation strat-egy. These plans explicitly link a unit's growth objectives to its people development, so the company won't be sur-prised by any deficits. Barbara Simpson, HSBC's group head of talent, works closely with each unit to develop its proposal and presents the aggregated plans to the group head office, highlighting any gaps in talent to meet the firm's growth objectives. This process keeps talent man-agement high on the agendas of line and corporate leaders and prevents them from getting distracted by seemingly more pressing problems. What's more, talent management, succession planning, international moves, and senior-executive development are standing agenda items at meetings of business executive committees and the group's board.

The bank fosters engagement in new hires by sending them to the United Kingdom for a seven-week training program, typically in groups of 30 to 40, whose members represent about 20 nations. At these sessions, held sev-eral times a year, new employees have a chance not just to meet one another and members of the leadership team—Green or his most senior colleagues spend some time with them—but also to share their own ideas about the bank.

ENSURING ACCOUNTABILITY

Talent factories hold all stakeholders (including talented employees themselves) accountable for doing their part to make systems and processes robust. At P&G, Lafley claims ownership for career planning of all the general managers and vice presidents and for the talent pools that comprise what he refers to as the company's "top 16s": P&G's preeminent 16 markets, 16 customers, and 16 brands. He reviews the top talent assignment and succession plans for each business and region annually. Along with the company's vice chairs and presidents, he personally sponsors and teaches all the leadership development courses for the company's most senior 300 leaders, signaling that talent management is both a leadership responsibility and a core business process. All of P&G's managers and executives understand that they will be held accountable for identifying and developing the firm's current and future leaders. They are evaluated and compensated on their contributions to building organizational competence, not just on their performance.

HSBC's Green holds his group management board, which comprises about a dozen executives, accountable for the company's talent pools. Each member is responsible for a region, a customer group, or a product. Members oversee the list of people in their own business in the regional talent pool as well and select managers for the group pool.

Executives are also held accountable for maintaining honesty in the talent management process, which is easier said than done, says Green. "We've had people who got into talent pools who shouldn't have. You can either let it ride, or you have that hard conversation saying, 'Sorry, this wasn't right,' or 'You were a legitimate member of the talent pool but you started to coast and lost it a bit.' You don't do people a favor by being nice all the time."

LEADERS HAVE LONG SAID that people are their companies' most important assets, but making the most of them has acquired a new urgency. Any company aiming to grow—and, in particular, to grow on the global stage—has little hope of achieving its goals without the ability to put the right people on the ground, and fast. Companies apply focus and drive toward capital, information technology, equipment, and world-class processes, but in the end, it's the people who matter most.

Originally published in June 2007
Reprint R0706D

How to Keep
A Players Productive

STEVEN BERGLAS

Executive Summary

AFTER GRADUATING from Harvard Business School with
highest honors, Jane rapidly moved up the corporate ladder at a large advertising firm, racking up promotions and
responsibilities along the way. By the time she became the
company's creative director, she was, in everyone's estimation, an A player—one of the organization's most gifted
and productive employees. But although she received an
extraordinarily generous pay package and had what
some people considered to be one of the most stimulating
jobs in the company, Jane felt underappreciated and
was talking to headhunters. Eventually, she was lured
away to a competing company that, by her own admission, offered less-challenging work. Both Jane and the
advertising firm she left behind lost out.

Of course, not all A players are as vulnerable as
Jane. Some superstars soar to stunning heights, needing

little or no special attention, and have the natural self-confidence and brilliance to stay at the top of their game with elegance and grace. But as every manager knows, megastars with manageable egos are rare. Far more common are people like Jane who are striving to satisfy an inner need for recognition that is often a sign of irrationally low self-esteem.

According to the author—an executive coach, management consultant, and former faculty member of the department of psychiatry at Harvard Medical School—if you do not carefully manage the often unconscious need A players have for kudos and appreciation, they will burn out in a way that is damaging to them and unproductive for you. The key is understanding what makes your A players tick. The author suggests that you assist your stars by offering them authentic praise, helping them set boundaries, and teaching them to play nicely with subordinates. In the process, you can turn these high performers into even more effective players.

AFTER GRADUATING from Harvard Business School with highest honors, Jane rapidly moved up the corporate ladder at a large advertising firm, racking up promotions and responsibilities all along the way. By the time she became the company's creative director, she was, in everyone's estimation, an "A player"—one of the organization's most gifted and productive employees. But although she received an extraordinarily generous pay package and had what some people considered to be one of the most stimulating jobs in the company, Jane was talking to headhunters behind the scenes.

Jane's problem was that she felt underappreciated. She consistently overperformed, and her boss said she did great work. This was the highest accolade he ever gave anyone, but Jane needed more. She worked harder and harder, but more fulsome praise never came her way. Her boss's inability to amply reward her achievement was exasperating. Eventually, she was lured away to a competing company that, by her own admission, offered less challenging work. Both Jane and the advertising firm she left behind lost out.

Not all A players are as vulnerable as Jane. Some superstars soar to stunning heights needing little or no special attention. They have the natural self-confidence and brilliance to stay at the top of their game with elegance and grace. Of course, these are your most prized employees, and they pose their own challenges and risks. (See the insert "Nobody's Perfect" at the end of this article.) But as every manager knows, megastars with manageable egos are rare. Far more common are people like Jane who are striving to satisfy an inner need for recognition that is often a sign of irrationally low self-esteem. If you do not carefully manage the often unconscious needs of these A players for kudos and appreciation, they will burn out in a way that is damaging to themselves and unproductive for you.

Certainly, managers aren't therapists or executive coaches, and they don't have to be. But it will help your organization if you try to understand what makes your A players tick. In my work with more than 30 CEOs, a dozen COOs, and nearly as many law firm managing partners, I have observed persistent patterns among superachievers that can give you valuable insight into how to manage them and their careers. In the following article, I will explore the psychology and behaviors of A players and suggest some ways that you can turn your high performers into even more effective stars.

The Superior Worm

When we think of A players, a fairly consistent picture comes to mind for most of us. A players are the people with the "right stuff." They are the most fiercely ambitious, wildly capable, and intelligent people in any organization. Yet despite their veneer of self-satisfaction, smugness, and even bluster, a significant number of your spectacular performers suffer from a lack of confidence. Ron Daniel, a former managing director of McKinsey & Company, the blue-chip management consulting firm, made the point when he told *Fortune* that "The real competition out there isn't for clients, it's for people. And we look to hire people who are first, very smart; second, insecure and thus driven by their insecurity; and third, competitive." Translated, many A players are insecure overachievers. They're often the people who went to the right schools and who pushed themselves to win all the prizes. But if they are so smart and competitive, why are they so insecure?

In my observation of many A players, I have concluded that childhood really matters. Often these high performers come from demanding backgrounds where unconditional approval was withheld. Getting As, for example, did not meet with admiration from parents. The achievement was typically followed up with the message, "You can do better," which is never rewarding and often damaging. From your star's perspective, feedback of this sort obligated him to work endlessly to reach an unattainable goal. The psychologist Anna Freud

(Sigmund Freud's daughter) and others who studied children raised in this manner discovered that these individuals end up with extraordinarily punishing superegos. At first, the pressure comes from outside authority figures; later, A players impose it on themselves and on others. Winston Churchill, who adored his often abusive father, is a case in point. As an adult, Churchill ended each day with a merciless ritual: "I try myself by court martial to see if I have done anything effective during the day."

Churchill is not alone. A players often assume the parental role and end up voluntarily pushing themselves to extremes, producing more and better work in every endeavor they undertake. I once knew a high achiever from a prominent law firm. When he got his annual review, he turned out to be the leading performer among his cohorts. His superiors described his work as excellent and superb, but rather than rejoice in having received such amazing accolades, the attorney worried aloud to his wife that his work was sometimes described as merely excellent rather than superb. This intense concern with the precise language of praise sounds strange and self-absorbed to most people, particularly when a prized employee is essentially drawing the distinction between an A+ and an A++ evaluation. But vulnerable stars are highly attentive to the language of the person judging them precisely because they spent their childhoods looking intently for clues about whether or not they had fulfilled parental expectations.

What do people get out of such self-defeating behavior? The psychologist Alfred Adler, the man who brought inferiority and superiority complexes into our everyday language, offered an explanation almost 100 years ago. Adler argued that the most fundamental human need is for superiority, a need that arises from universal feelings of inferiority experienced by us all in early childhood when we are helpless and dependent on others. If we manage these feelings appropriately, we go on to lead well-adjusted lives. But if powerful authority figures thwart our efforts to overcome these feelings, then complexes develop, causing narcissistic grandiosity that can linger for the rest of our lives. Adler asserted that if a person suffers either from an inferiority or a superiority complex (which for Adler were opposite sides of the same coin), then whatever he achieves it will never be enough. As I once heard it put: "Some people go through life feeling superior; others go through life feeling like worms. Narcissists go through life feeling like superior worms." One might assume that A players' feelings of superiority are a tremendous boon to them since, among other things, these feelings help them to communicate enormous self-confidence to others. But the plight of the overachiever who feels like a superior worm is that he must live with the constant anxiety that he might in fact be inferior to others. Only when you can help your stars address their inflated senses of superiority can they begin to deal with underlying issues of poor self-worth.

Can't Say No

One of the biggest challenges for A players is their inability to set boundaries for themselves. Ordinary people usually know how to step back from situations where vague requests make them uncomfortable; but insecure overachievers typically exceed expectations because they are prepared to operate outside their comfort zones in their efforts to win recognition. When given an ambigu-

ous request such as "I need directions to Rome," they will
not only provide a map of all roads leading to Rome but
also give you all air routes, water routes, and railway
routes as well—just as any overachiever would. I know
one superstar who was asked to find a few examples of
the best insurance policies that the company had produced in the last five years. He didn't conclude his
research until he had reviewed every policy the company
had written in the last 25 years. While overextensions
such as these may be impressive, they are not always a
productive use of time. Additionally, when word of such
efforts spreads across the organization, it can cause
unnecessary disruption as other high performers feel
that they, too, have to overachieve to such extremes to
get the attention they need.

If you think about your stars' unconscious motiva-
tions, this overeagerness to please makes a lot of sense.
People raised in an environment where praise was carefully meted out typically do not try to challenge the rules;
they follow them. When presented with a request that he
thinks is unreasonable or unclear, the A player is most
likely just to back down and try to comply rather than to
question authority. That makes your superstar particularly dependent on powerful figures in situations that
subject him to unclear directions or sudden shifts in the
rules. Since A players have tried to appease influential
people all their lives in order to "know" how to behave,
they are not prepared to follow through appropriately on
requests that are not straightforward.

For a case in point, consider Jack, a rising star at a
prestigious consulting firm, and an A player in terms of
his dazzling brilliance and drive. (Not all A players are
men, but the problem A players I have worked with are
mostly men.) When one of the directors asked Jack to

chair an important research project that the firm was
conducting, Jack pushed his team to produce a report
that was considerably in excess of anything the other
research teams had done. When he hinted to the director
that he didn't get the recognition he deserved, his supervisor responded, "Nobody asked you to do all that work."
A more savvy boss would have understood that Jack's
inability to set boundaries was a problem he needed
help with, and he certainly would not have added fuel to
the fire.

In some situations, of course, that kind of over-
achievement is built into a company's business model.
Blue-chip law firms, management consultancies, and
investment banks offer huge salaries and great opportunities for A players in exchange for agonizingly back-
breaking work. But in these professional firms, everyone
recognizes the deal. Such companies rely on churning
out A players and constantly replacing them with
recruits from the top business and graduate schools, who
are more than eager to join these prestigious firms. It
makes for a highly productive workforce. In the best of
all possible worlds, the experienced A player moves on to
greener pastures before he suffers burnout. When he
goes, the firm has benefited from the services of a spectacular achiever, and the A player leaves with another
superb credential on his CV.

This business model, however, does not apply to the
vast majority of companies that find it hard to attract
A players and that need to retain them in order to fight
for, and maintain, competitive edge. In these organizations, the failure of stars to set boundaries will almost
certainly lead them to walk out in frustration or rage.
Unfortunately, unless your company is a McKinsey or a

Goldman Sachs, you will have to struggle more to replace these star performers.

The Dissing Dan

The A Player is usually very comfortable keeping company with his boss, which is obviously an asset to him in his career (and to his boss). He is likely to have developed this ease with authority figures early in life, by first appeasing a demanding parent. Later, the star usually becomes a teacher's pet who grows into a company man or woman and maintains a capacity for pleasing those who are higher up.

Sadly, such people usually don't get to capitalize on the goodwill they earn with their bosses because their hidden vulnerabilities often make them hostile to those hierarchically below them (whom they usually regard as being less able). Indeed, spectacular performers will often actively shun interactions with juniors if not directed to work with them in an amicable manner. Even then, they may not. This attitude creates havoc for the superstar as he interacts with subordinates. Often, he views them with disdain and finds endless reasons to criticize their work. In turn, they get defensive and fight back against the criticism, which only serves to make him react even more arrogantly in an attempt to bolster his ego. He will, for example, not only point out a current flaw but also go back months to chronicle a litany of mistakes that suggest his colleagues are routinely second-rate. This creates a vicious cycle that has derailed many a star performer's career because in time superiors recognize that the A player is repeatedly manufacturing ill will in otherwise functional teams.

Consider a vice president in an advertising agency who acquired the nickname Dissing Dan because of his disrespect for his subordinates. A high performer greatly valued by his superiors, Dan would subtly dismiss junior members of the company, undercutting them with irony and wit. At the team's weekly meeting, for example, Dan dominated the show, criticizing the ideas of other team members. Immediately after the meetings, however, he dashed off memos to the executive vice presidents, claiming the team's best ideas for himself.

Thanks to Dan, every senior manager in the company kept abreast of the newest thinking in the company. But when it became obvious to his teammates that he was grabbing credit for their work, they demanded a new leader. Dan was allowed to complete his current project, but his reputation for being condescending to the "little people" had spread across the company and many subordinates refused to work with him. In the end, his contemptuous attitude toward juniors turned out to be less a problem for managers than a career killer for him. When an opportunity for advancement presented itself, Dan was passed over and his career stalled.

Managing Their Insecurities

The good news for bosses coping with complicated A players is that managing superstars is not as difficult as it seems. The biggest challenge is simply recognizing that these driven stars have these hidden vulnerabilities. Once you've understood their unexpected weaknesses and needs, you can apply some straightforward guidelines and techniques to help them overcome their limitations.

LET THEM TRIUMPH

In dealing with stars, you should always begin by searching your own emotions about them. It can be hard to
manage people with the talent, intellect, and imagina-
tion that A players possess and not be envious of them.
Their apparent self-confidence makes the task even
harder. But you have to recognize and control your own
emotions if want to manage your high achievers effectively. In their desire to impress, A players can easily
push your buttons. I recall sitting in a finance committee
meeting once where a dazzling high achiever, the
comptroller, kept interrupting the CFO to inject his
expertise. When the meeting ended, the comptroller
looked toward the CFO for kudos. Instead, the CFO
turned to me and said, "It's hard to appreciate genius,
even when you know that you need genius to get the
job done."

That's not to say you should let your A players ride
roughshod over you. There are times when you have to
push back: You're the manager, and it's up to you to set
an overall strategy for your company or unit and to make
sure that each individual is contributing to the benefit of
all. The challenge is working out just when your conces-
sions to the stars will help or hurt the team. Usually, you
can give in quite a lot before you have to stop conceding.
The best sports coaches, for example, often give in to the
stars on practically all the little things, and the stars
show their appreciation by being extra willing to follow
the coach's strategy. In business, satisfied stars will
reward you by attracting other stars to the team. Everyone wants to be associated with winning people or
teams. In this way, your top performers can become the

organization's best salespeople if you can successfully manage their grandiose needs.

PRAISE PERSONALLY, PRAISE OFTEN

Because they did not get the right sort of praise at an appropriate stage in their emotional development, your stars have difficulty internalizing the good things they hear, and so they need to hear them spoken again and again. Of course, you will grow weary of having to reassure your most valuable player every day that he is number one and will be tempted to dish out the same old "atta boy." But generic praise will not do. A players are not fooled by false accolades; they crave discerning praise in order to attain their unconscious goal of genuine self-esteem. As a manager, the onus falls on you to personalize your praise if it is to be effective.

Personalizing praise means knowing not only when but *what* to honor when considering your star employee's spectacular performance. You must celebrate the unique competencies and aspirations that the A player values in herself, and you must admire her in a way that she can appreciate. Whatever you do, you must make sure that your praise is authentic. This is crucial when dealing with A players because they view those who evaluate their work with a jaundiced eye. They crave praise, but unless it is sincere and tailored to them, they suspect that it is fabricated and dismiss it out of hand.

Communicating authenticity is relatively easy to do: Avoid hyperbole, clichés, and platitudes. But determining how best to tailor your praise is much more difficult. Each A player has dispositions that make her either receptive or unreceptive to various forms of social interactions. When a boss calls someone into his office to tell her that her job is safe, for example, it's quite likely that the person will conclude that the boss had thought of firing her. You don't need to be a trained psychotherapist to see this danger. However, you do have to recognize that you must spend extra time observing your star players and listening to their special needs. Some players want to be in the limelight, so praise them publicly. Others need you to appreciate a personal quirk; don't hold back on your approval. Sometimes it can help for you to articulate to yourself what you most admire about your stars. If you do that, you will come very close to knowing what they need to have recognized and praised. Many managers are often afraid that giving such personalized praise will overindulge an A player, turning a productive narcissist into an uncontrollable prima donna. While there is some risk of that, in my observation withholding praise only alienates your key players, making them even less likely to be effective team players than they might otherwise have been.

Even managers who do work hard to give personalized praise may, over time, subtly raise the bar on their superachievers unfairly. It's a trap I call "success tolerance." Just as drug or alcohol abusers develop a tolerance to intoxicants and need ever-increasing dosages of a drug to achieve highs, managers develop a tolerance to the stellar work of their superstars. At first your megastar's performance inspires your awe and admiration. Eventually, however, you will come to expect that level of achievement from your star and see it as an average performance from her. For you to react to her work with, "Wow, Jennifer, terrific job," the superstar will have to up her dose of already superb performance to a level that is off the charts. This happens to everyone in organizations, but the problem is particularly acute for superachieving A players who are already eagerly seeking your praise.

The only antidote to success tolerance is to become aware of the tendency in yourself and to fight against it. One technique is to broaden the scope of your praise. For example, if you have an A player HR officer who is in charge of preparing your corporation for the upcoming demographic shock precipitated by aging baby boomers, compliment her from time to time for work she does outside of her immediate domain. This satisfies her need for kudos while avoiding praise inflation with respect to her core job.

SET CLEAR BOUNDARIES

Given an A player's drive to please authority figures in order to secure praise, it has to be up to the authority figures to put a cap or outer limit on performance expectations. Stars are simply incapable of setting their own boundaries. As any executive coach will tell you, stars who walk out of their jobs because of burnout nearly always get themselves into the same difficulties in their next jobs—unless they are lucky enough to find a boss who knows how to manage them. (See the insert "Superstar Burnout" at the end of this article.)

A good way to set boundaries is to allow your A players to help you build work groups, structure a project, or tailor a business plan. Then—and this is the critical point—ask them how they would like to be rewarded for completing those subtasks. By working with a star in this manner, you are not handing over the reins of strategic management of your department. You are negotiating a kind of contract with him.

Another useful tactic to help your A players develop boundaries is a variation of a psychotherapeutic technique that forces an individual to gain insight into her behavior. Rather than overtly asking, "Why did you kill yourself over that?" a manager might say, "Who asked you to do all this work?" From a psychodynamic point of view, the answer to the question *should be* "my parents." But since no one expects a superstar to have been through intensive psychotherapy, she'll probably say, "Well, you did." The skilled manager should then respond, "I'll see to it that I never push you to such extreme performance standards again. I thought I had set the bar lower. What did I say that made you feel that I hadn't?" In all such interventions, there must be dialogue about expectations. A manager has to communicate to his star performers that he doesn't want them to burn out. In this way, a manager will help his A players understand that they don't have to outperform themselves time and again. Indeed, it is precisely the perfectionist, overachieving A player who can benefit from G.K. Chesterton's wise counsel: "If a thing is worth doing, it is worth doing badly." While such advice would be disastrous for your B and C players, it is motivating for your superstar who is already going above and beyond the call of duty.

MAKE THEM PLAY NICE

Bosses must create an environment where top performers have to cooperate with other people in order to achieve their goals. That will certainly mean building the notion of shared effort into an A player's performance measures. At the same time, you must set realistic expectations for what you can achieve in this respect: Even seasoned psychotherapists recognize that the best that therapy has to offer is an amelioration of symptoms. Phobias, for example, are not cured; they are brought under control. Likewise, when dealing with A players, you should not expect them to feel warmly toward less talented people.

The process that coaches call "surrendering the 'me' for the 'we' " is not easy to convey to A players who have not participated in team activities before. For these individuals, a more effective means of getting them to play along may be to repeatedly highlight the failures of other superstars, such as those of NBA player Bob McAdoo, who, despite his exceptional talent and many awards, almost ended his sports career with a reputation for not being a team player. This approach exposes your A players to the downside of too much self-reliance without making it personal. You never want to hold an A player's own shortcomings up for inspection in public because that would magnify his insecurities and drive him from your organization. But by carefully exposing a vulnerable star to what I call "sympathetic failure experiences," you can create enough awareness in most high achievers to have them see the benefits of "using"—if not fully embracing—members of their team to their advantage. Here, again, do not expect a megastar to exhibit true camaraderie; this is not the goal of the intervention. You can, however, modify his overt behavior toward subordinates if he sees that the consequences of going it alone can be more painful than following, however begrudgingly, the agendas of a group effort.

This brings me to a final tactic that great sports coaches reliably use to manage their superstars: They co-opt them. Great coaches often make star talent junior coaches to the team. This philosophy of asking stars to coach rather than mentor subordinates is that it does not ask an A player to come down to the level of a junior; rather, it raises your flawed star to your level and invites him to perform at a higher status. In their heart of hearts, narcissistic A players just don't have a yen for advancing the careers of juniors in an organization. No one remembers the names of great mentors, so asking your megastars to become big brothers or big sisters to colleagues will not appear rewarding to them. They want to surround themselves with other A players and to be seen as first among *them*. They also aspire to succeed their bosses. Indeed, an overachiever might view his elevated position as a signal that he is being groomed for the top spot. In fact, he may well be. If he performs well as a coach, that performance may improve his chances of subsequent promotions. When that logic computes into his calculus, he is usually more willing to "go along to get along" with the rest of the organization.

Sooner or later, most managers will have to deal with an A player who is difficult to manage. You may be thinking, why not drop these stars and try to create a fully functioning team of A− and B+ players? The answer is not so simple. Even your flawed A players have an enormous amount to offer your organization. Research shows that 80% of a business's profits are generated by 20% of its workers—in other words, by these high-achieving A players. Of course, sometimes your stars will not be worth all your time and effort, and you'll have to encourage them to look for opportunities elsewhere—both for their own good and for the good of your organization. But in most cases, A players can make a huge difference to the bottom line. If you manage them well, you can multiply that value to your organization many times over.

Nobody's Perfect

BECAUSE I AM HIRED by companies to work with supertalented A players who have problems, I do not typically coach what I call the "well-oiled wheels." These A players move through organizations with grace, achievement, and, most significantly, little inner torment. I doubt that these individuals have ever seen the inside of a psychiatrist's office and trust they never will. However, this does not mean they do not have specific needs or areas of professional development that require nurturing. Although those needs are few and easily addressed, it is wise to make doing so a top priority since these are the A players you can least afford to lose to the competition.

Smart But Not Savvy

Because your well-oiled A players will not behave in ways that call for you to mentor them like insecure A players (unlike insecure overachievers, they don't violate boundaries), you may forget that they will be on a career trajectory that puts them in business settings that demand social skills they may not be prepared to handle. Like a child who skips grades in elementary school and is a 13-year-old high school senior with no idea how to act at a prom, an A player might be moved along a career path in ways that prevent him from developing interpersonal skills. In law, the practice of having associates serve as second chairs provides novice litigators guidance about how to develop the social skills needed to behave in court. Having a well-oiled A player be your second chair whenever you meet with customers or clients will allow him to observe the manner in which a professional deals effectively with others. As a result, he will gain invaluable skills.

Tolerant But Not Collegial

Although well-oiled A players are not hostile toward juniors the way insecure A players are, it is doubtful that they consider B and C players their colleagues. Like insecure A players, they, too, were teachers' pets throughout their formative years and were more comfortable relating to authority figures. Consequently, as they become ready to assume managerial positions, they find that they are unable to form peer networks at the very point in their careers when doing so matters most. Given their lack of inner turmoil, however, well-oiled A players will usually have little difficulty serving as mentors to others. For this reason, I advise using them whenever possible to coach C players who need help mastering tasks. The literature on mentoring demonstrates that one result of mentoring is the development of an intimate bond between mentor and mentee. Soon, your A players will develop a network of friendly work relationships as a result of their tutoring.

Ambitious But Not Challenged

The only occasions when I have been called in to coach well-oiled A players is when they were suffering burnout born of midcareer boredom. All fast-track careers slow down. You rise rapidly, your pay goes up quickly, you sprint ahead of the cohort with whom you were hired. But after a point, the curve starts to flatten. (For more on this topic, see Robert Morison, Tamara Erickson, and Ken Dychtwald, "Managing Middlescence," HBR March 2006.) That is the exhilarating nature of a horse race: running from the gate, jockeying for position around the first turn, and then running for the lead. However, if you are three furlongs ahead of the pack, the long, long straightaway down the backstretch is mind-numbing. For A players accustomed to action and rewards, this long backstretch is fraught with danger; there's less that is new, and boredom can set in. The only answer to this dilemma is to provide these individuals with challenges. It is almost impossible to overload well-oiled A players if you collaborate with them on defining the nature of a challenge. They will approach such growth opportunities with passion. If you don't provide them, someone else will.

Superstar Burnout

"BURNOUT" IS A TERM that is imprecise and difficult to define, but we know it when we see it. Christina Maslach, a pioneer in the field of burnout research, described the phenomenon as a syndrome of emotional exhaustion and cynicism characterized by symptoms ranging from chronic fatigue and anger to a sense of feeling trapped in a job that has ceased to have personal meaning.

A players who feel burned out or underappreciated at one corporation often think they can solve the problem by changing jobs. Yet when your prized performer transfers to what he expects will be a problem-free arena—when he takes what psychologists call a "geographic cure"—he gambles that the new location will prove a panacea for all his past woes. Chances are good that he will take his problems with him. Indeed, geographic cures can even exacerbate the sufferer's symptoms. If he moves to Eden and his symptoms don't change as a result of that Garden's magical influence, he can only infer that his disease has worsened! Take the case of John, a broker from a Boston investment firm whom I treated when I was at Harvard Medical School. A hedge fund manager, John came to me when his wife threatened to leave him because of his long hours on the job. He acknowledged that she had a point. He was only 38, no longer felt gratified by his multimillion dollar income, and knew he was only working to earn kiss-off money. While he said he hoped psychotherapy could help him, he never invested in it fully. Instead, he and a team of colleagues formed their own hedge fund, which John thought would give him more control over his life. To mollify his wife, he began attending his son's Little League games, promising to take a more active role in the things his boy loved.

Eighteen months after he finished psychotherapy and initiated a geographic cure from his old brokerage firm, John had to admit to himself that his attempt to avoid burnout was a total failure. Starting his own hedge fund involved harder work and longer hours. His attempt to become a Little League dad had backfired, too. He suspected that things were flying out of control when he began looking into the idea of purchasing a home stadium for his son's Little League team. Eventually, John began to abuse prescription drugs for relief from his anxieties. When his fellow partners staged an intervention, he was forced to enter rehab.

Like John, other A players who suffer burnout often start acting out, expressing their inner conflict in some form of destructive behavior—be it extramarital affairs, chemical dependencies, or gambling disorders. However disruptive this behavior may be for an organization, it can serve the sufferer well: The emotionally exhausted A player is no longer expected to live up to expectations until his problem is resolved. In addition, he may gain extra nurturing and attention from authority figures.

Originally published in September 2006
Reprint R0609F

Managing Middlescence

ROBERT MORISON, TAMARA J. ERICKSON,
AND KEN DYCHTWALD

Executive Summary

THEY MAKE UP more than half your workforce. They
work longer hours than anyone else in your company.
From their ranks come most of your top managers.
They're your midcareer employees, the solid citizens
between the ages of 35 and 55 whom you bank on for
their loyalty and commitment. And they're not happy.

In fact, they're burned out, bored, and bottlenecked,
new research reveals. Only 33% of the 7,700 workers
the authors surveyed feel energized by their work; 36%
say they're in dead-end jobs. One in three is not satisfied
with his or her job. One in five is looking for another.

Welcome to *middlescence*. Like adolescence, it can
be a time of frustration, confusion, and alienation. But it
can also be a time of self-discovery, new direction, and
fresh beginnings. Today, millions of midcareer men and
women are wrestling with middlescence—looking for

ways to balance work, family, and leisure while hoping to find new meaning in their jobs. The question is, Will they find it in your organization or elsewhere?

Companies are ill prepared to manage middlescence because it is so pervasive, largely invisible, and culturally uncharted. That neglect is bad for business: Many companies risk losing some of their best people or—even worse—ending up with an army of disaffected people who stay.

The best way to engage middlescents is to tap into their hunger for renewal and help them launch into more meaningful roles. Perhaps managers can't grant a promotion to everyone who merits one in today's flat organizations, but you may be able to offer new training, fresh assignments, mentoring opportunities, even sabbaticals or entirely new career paths within your own company.

Millions of midcareer men and women would like nothing better than to convert their restlessness into fresh energy. They just need the occasion—and perhaps a little assistance—to unleash and channel all that potential.

Burned-out, bottlenecked, and bored. That's the current lot of millions of midcareer employees. In our research into employee attitudes and experiences, we heard many stories of midcareer restlessness, a phenomenon we call *middlescence*. There was the manager who was beginning to realize that he'd never become the company president, the senior executive who felt that she had sacrificed her life—and her spirit—for her job, and the technician who was bored stiff with his unchallenging assignments. Typical is the case of one produc-

tive and well-respected middle manager in his late forties. He was sandwiched between obligations at the
office and at home, and his work group was demoralized
after two rounds of downsizing. The company's structure
had flattened, leaving fewer possibilities than ever for
promotion, and he felt stalled. "This isn't how my life and
career were supposed to play out," he told the employee
counselor. "I don't know how much longer I can cope."

Like adolescence, middlescence can be a time of frustration, confusion, and alienation but also a time of self-
discovery, new direction, and fresh beginnings. Today,
millions of midcareer men and women are wrestling with
middlescence—looking for ways to balance job responsibilities, family, and leisure while hoping to find new
meaning in their work.

Midcareer employees—those between the ages of 35
and 54—make up more than half the workforce. One in
four has managerial or supervisory responsibility. When
in June 2004 we at Age Wave and the Concours Group
conducted a survey with Harris Interactive of more than
7,700 U.S. workers, we found that people in this age
bracket work longer hours than their older and younger
counterparts, with 30% saying they put in 50 or more
hours per week. Yet only 43% are passionate about their
jobs, just 33% feel energized by their work, 36% say they
feel that they are in dead-end jobs, and more than 40%
report feelings of burnout.

Midcareer employees are the least likely to say that
their workplace is congenial and fun or that it offers
ample opportunity to try new things. As a group, they
have the lowest satisfaction rates with their immediate
managers and the least confidence in top executives.
Only one in three agrees that top management displays

integrity or commitment to employee development, and one in four often disagrees with the organization's policies on important employee matters. A fifth are seeking opportunities in other organizations, and a similar percentage are looking for a major career change. But 85% believe that career changes are very difficult these days. Family and financial pressures outside work make them conservative in their career choices, and many cannot afford moves that would involve cuts in pay or benefits. Other research has yielded similar findings: According to a 2005 Conference Board survey, the largest decline in job satisfaction over the past ten years occurred among workers between the ages of 35 and 44, and the second largest decline was among those aged 45 to 54. In short, far too many midcareer employees are working more, enjoying it less, and looking for alternatives.

The Problems

Middlescent restlessness isn't new, but it plays out differently in different generations. It seems to be hitting today's midcareer workers harder than it hit their predecessors. Increased longevity, delayed (and multiple) marriages, and large numbers of two-career households have altered family patterns such that middlescents are often sandwiched at home between raising children and caring for aging parents precisely at the time when their job responsibilities are peaking. Increased longevity also means that the average 50 year old today could be looking forward to 30 years or more of healthy, active life. That can be a blessing—time enough to learn new skills, start another career, build an entrepreneurial business, or shift priorities to give back to society. Or it can be a curse—for those without the financial resources to chart their own course, who instead face the prospect of having to work indefinitely at a job they don't really enjoy. Either way, it's a problem for their current employers.

Generationally, most of today's (and all of the older) midcareer employees are baby boomers, their values forged in the midst of the Vietnam War, Watergate, and the civil rights and women's rights movements. In middlescence many are asking themselves: Have I had the impact I expected to have? How can I make the next phase of my life as meaningful as possible? Earlier generations looked to their work for security and material success; the way to combat restlessness was usually to hunker down and focus on one's current job. Many of today's idealistic yet frustrated boomers have different goals—they'd be willing to trade some of their current success for greater significance in their lives and work, even if that means doing something altogether different.

Companies are ill-prepared to manage middlescence because it is so pervasive, largely invisible, and culturally uncharted. Many midcareer men and women may crave a fresh start but don't tell their bosses how they feel (see the insert "Sources of Frustration" at the end of this article). Employers view these people as solid corporate citizens, bank on their loyalty and commitment, and assume they're doing fine.

That neglect is bad for business: Many companies risk losing some of their best people, who may opt for early retirement or seek more exciting work elsewhere. Firms are too often blindsided when valuable people up and quit. We met, for instance, with executives at an aerospace company that had recently lost a midcareer technical manager who wanted to grow but couldn't see any near term possibilities for advancement. His bosses knew this but did nothing, so the employee left to start his own consulting firm. In retrospect, the executives recognized that they could have easily found ways to make his job more interesting and challenging. As it is, they're hoping he'll eventually return.

Also bad for business are the many disaffected people who stay. Every day that an employee is less than fully engaged in his or her work, the company pays a price—a loss of energy and enthusiasm, a lack of innovation and focus. We have become convinced that the problem of burned-out, turned-off employees who stay is even more threatening to corporate productivity than the problem of turnover.

In the years ahead, both tangible talent shortages and growing disengagement from work will present unprecedented challenges to business productivity and growth. In our March 2004 HBR article, "It's Time to Retire Retirement," we wrote of strategies to combat the coming brain drain, as the vanguard of baby boomers approaches retirement age. But the solution to talent shortages doesn't lie in enticing just one generation of older workers to continue contributing; rather, companies need to make working past retirement (at least part-time) the norm from now on. That means making current work more enjoyable and enriching, because the way to retain your middlescents for the long haul is to reengage them today.

The best way to do so is to tap into their hunger for renewal and help them launch into new, more productive, more meaningful roles and careers. Millions of mid-career men and women would like nothing better than to convert their restlessness into fresh energy. They just need the occasion, and perhaps a little assistance, to unleash and channel all that potential energy. Chances are, you're already using some of the career revitalization techniques we'll recommend, but we'll wager you're focusing them mainly on your company's stars. It's time to apply them to the much broader, and too often neglected, constituency of midcareer employees.

Six Strategies for Revitalizing Careers

You may not be able to offer everybody more money or a prestigious title, but you can give just about anybody a fresh challenge or a new start. As many of our examples show, the most successful careers are the ones that stay in motion.

You must, however, take two preliminary steps to prepare the ground. First, you need to *remove the barriers* to occupational mobility. Such barriers take many forms. Policies (formal or tacit) regarding required time in role between job changes may be too strict. Your organization may have a job-posting system but still fill most openings through under-the-table recruiting that bypasses official channels. Your company may be tacitly unwilling, or even unconsciously disinclined, to invest in extensive training for employees over a certain age. Managers may get away with blocking employees from new assignments, and policies forbidding such behavior may be enforced loosely, at best. And employees themselves may perceive role changes, career redirections, new training, lateral moves, and flexible work arrangements as signs of inadequacy or failure.

Second, be sure to *find the keepers.* If you can identify high potentials through your performance management system, then surely you can also identify the next tier down. You want to go beyond the stars (who are probably getting special attention already) to find the other valuable contributors—the B players, people who will probably never make it to the executive suite but whose skills and experience you need to retain. These are the people you'd like to see eventually moving into flex retirement, not full retirement. Once you've identified them, pay special attention not only to their potential, performance, and progress but also to any warning signs of middlescent disillusionment and stagnation.

To help you keep those keepers, we've identified six fundamental tools.

FRESH ASSIGNMENTS

A fresh assignment, often in a different geographical location or part of the organization, lets you take advantage of a person's existing skills, experience, and contacts while letting him or her develop new ones. The best assignments are often lateral moves that mix roughly equal parts old and new responsibilities.

During our interviews, for example, we met with Jeff Kimpan, a longtime HR executive at General Motors. He worked in Mexico during the mid-1980s, a period of explosive growth there. Then he joined the executive ranks, most recently running HR for worldwide manufacturing operations. In the spring of 2005, the HR director for the company's fast-growing China operation quit, and Jeff volunteered for the job. It was actually a step down in corporate status and scope, and his colleagues were shocked that he'd accept what seemed a less than lateral move. He acknowledges that he had to check his ego, but he was ready for a change, and he knew that he could apply what he'd learned 20 years earlier in Mexico. His children were grown, and he was excited about getting away from restructurings and downsizings to work in a growing business.

It isn't an easy job. The China operation hopes to double its sales in two years and redouble in four, so the unit was already facing shortages of experienced technical and professional people when Jeff arrived. But he's having fun. "I can't wait to get to work each day," he says. "I come home just as tired as I did in Detroit—it's just a better kind of tired. This place is like a lab: Solutions aren't known, and they have to be invented every day. You'd have to be dead not to have fun in this job."

Principal Financial Group routinely chooses empty nesters like Jeff for relocation, particularly those moves that would be difficult for employees with young and growing families. So does GE, which also taps experienced managers to integrate new acquisitions—an ideal way to offer an employee a change of scene and bring to bear a career's worth of organizational know-how. Diana Tyson, who has spent 22 years in organizational development with AT&T and now Lucent Technologies, recently left corporate headquarters for a yearlong engagement in the fast-growing Asia-Pacific region. "After this experience, it would be a lot harder for another company to recruit me," she told us.

Marriott International's information resources group takes another innovative approach to the fresh assignment. Tenures there are long and turnover is low, which means high levels of competence but little potential for upward mobility. So senior managers have been offered opportunities to take on a second, lateral role, while offloading some of their current responsibilities, as a way to introduce new challenges. For example, Patton Conner, the vice president of guest services systems, recently took on a second "day job" as the regional VP for information resources of Marriott Canada. George Hall, a veteran human resources manager, is now also managing application development for the HR function. His new peers around the table are his customers in his other role, which he says gives him terrific insights into how to solve their problems. The more-junior employees who report to people like Patton and George have a chance to take on greater responsibility, since their bosses now have more to do in other areas.

Dow Chemical is one of the best examples we've seen of a company that has truly removed the barriers to career revitalization. Executives there assume that careers will always be in motion and that employees of all ages should always be preparing for their next career within the company. Dow backs up that expectation with tools that help people plan their next roles. One such is a career opportunity map that helps people determine which skills to acquire and which jobs to seek out. Another is a global job-posting system that alerts people to opportunities in other areas. It's a flat organization, so this approach allows the company to offer new and different work, even if it can't offer everyone a promotion.

Hewlett-Packard's Cathy Lyons has had a half-dozen very different assignments within the company over the past 12 years, from running a manufacturing operation in Italy to managing the U.S. toner supplies business to her most recent assignment as chief marketing officer at corporate headquarters. She believes that three or four years is long enough to be in any one position. "When you've stopped learning, it's time to move on or step aside," she told us.

CAREER CHANGES

Middlescents often dream of—and in some cases end up pursuing—something fundamentally new. Yet jumping the corporate ship is risky, so an employer that can offer an attractive internal career change has a chance to retain valuable talent. An employee may develop a new specialty, assume an altogether different job, or sometimes return from a management track to an individual contributor role.

Before joining Prudential Financial's Prudential Relocation business, Jim Russo spent 13 years with a major competitor in a customer relations role that kept him on the road. Looking for less travel and more time with his young family, Jim joined Prudential Relocation's new Phoenix office in 2000 as director of service delivery, managing a team of 21. The move was good for work/life balance, but after a while Jim became disenchanted: "The job wasn't my strength or my passion. I didn't feel as motivated, I missed working directly with customers, and I felt I was just getting the job done." By all measures, he was doing a good job, but he knew the situation wasn't right.

Jim liked the company and networked with a variety of managers to learn what kinds of opportunities there might be. He landed a position in field sales, a role for which he had no direct experience but which seemed to play to his strengths. The results—for Jim and the company—were beyond excellent. As sales director for the West Coast, he went up against his former employer. "I'm competitive by nature, and the job really fit," he says. "It gave me new life, more passion, more confidence, and companywide recognition—I know I'm a more important part of the company, and that really matters." In his first year, Jim was one of the top two salespeople; in his second, he tripled his sales target. His advice to others: "You've got to have passion for the job to add value every day. If you find yourself just going through the motions, do something different—perhaps very different. We all have strengths; find yours and play to them."

Such career shifts should be a natural part of corporate life. Dave Nassef has had three distinct careers in his 30-plus years with Pitney Bowes. He started as a personnel manager in a factory and made a lateral move to marketing. When the company centralized HR, he was one of the few people with both manufacturing and marketing experience, and at 40 he was given HR responsibility for half the company. He's since changed careers within the firm twice—first to take on the newly created job of corporate ombudsman and problem solver and then to move into the policy sphere, representing Pitney Bowes in Washington in legislative matters relating to the mailing industry. Each time, Dave surprised everyone around him with his willingness—eagerness, even—to make a lateral move. Dave's philosophy: "You have to ask yourself whether you want to thrive in a company or merely survive. If you want to thrive, then be prepared to take the risk of making a career change."

MENTORING COLLEAGUES

Putting experienced employees into mentoring, teaching, and other knowledge-sharing roles has the dual benefit of reengaging the midcareer worker and boosting the expertise and organizational know-how of less-experienced employees. For middlescents, serving as a mentor is a personally fulfilling way to share a lifetime of experience, give back to the organization, and make a fresh set of social connections in the workplace. Mentor relationships are often stereotyped as one-way transfers from old to young for the purposes of youthful personal development and career advancement. In fact, they should be viewed as a two-way pairing of knowledge to gain with knowledge to share.

That's how mentoring works at Intel, where the partner may outrank the mentor. The program began in a chip-making factory in New Mexico in 1997, when Intel was growing, and many of the factory's managers and technical experts were being transferred to new locations. New experts needed to be developed in a variety of fields. So the factory's top managers started matching partners with mentors who had the needed skills and knowledge. Today, a companywide employee database, which tracks skills attained and desired, helps match partners with mentors, who (thanks to the Internet) may be in another country. Both mentor and partner take a class to learn some guidelines—what to talk about, how to maximize the mutual benefit of their relationship— and then they set the details of that relationship in a contract that specifies goals and deadlines.

Mentoring is the best way to put the greatest number of midcareer workers into knowledge-sharing roles. But there are other ways. It's common practice for experienced and expert employees to develop and deliver training programs. They can also teach and guide colleagues through internal-consulting roles, participate in business performance reviews, and lead business improvement projects. Many midcareer workers are happy to take charge of change initiatives, which are especially appealing as a way to assist colleagues, improve results, and serve the higher mission of the enterprise.

FRESH TRAINING

Corporate training today is disproportionately aimed at the young (especially new employees who need to learn the basics) and at the high potentials. The tacit assumptions are that midcareer people have been trained already, and what little additional training they might need they get on the job. These assumptions are, at best, only partly true.

Many of today's midcareer workers are well educated and have retained their love of learning. They know that increasing their skills will raise their chances for personal and professional advancement. However, many find themselves too busy for extensive education and training; personal development time comes at the sacrifice of other responsibilities, both on the job and off. And some people, especially those who have reached positions of authority, stop seeking development opportunities because they hesitate to take risks or don't want to admit that they have things to learn.

Meanwhile, too many organizations foster a silent conspiracy against education: They cut the training and development budget first in lean times. They stand silent when managers discourage employees from seeking training on the grounds that it will interfere with getting the work done. And they fail to require managers to set career development plans for all their employees. As a result, many midcareer workers are overdue for a serious infusion of training—which can include refresher courses, in-depth education to develop new skills, and brief introductions to new ideas or areas of business that expand their perspectives and trigger their interest in learning more.

Fresh training is, of course, often integral to career changes as well as to employee retention. Lincoln Electric's Leopard Program, for instance, was designed explicitly to enable employees to "change their spots." When patterns of demand for steel fabrication products changed, the company trained dozens of factory and

clerical staff volunteers to become assistant salespeople.
In some Japanese manufacturers, assembly-line workers
regularly train to become product service technicians.
After years on the line, such employees literally know the
products inside and out, and probably want a change of
work. And the U.K.'s National Health Service is respond-
ing to chronic nursing shortages by training aides to
become nurses—a shift to a very different career path.

SABBATICALS

One of the best ways to rejuvenate, personally and pro-
fessionally, is simply to get away from the routine of the
job for a significant amount of time. A common feature
of academic employment relationships, sabbaticals
remain rare and underused in the business world. In
2001, Hewitt Associates surveyed more than 500 organizations in the United States and found that just 5%
offered sabbaticals, either paid or unpaid. Yet a survey
the same year by Principal Financial Group found that
more than 50% of employees say they long for a sabbatical but feel they can't take one because of financial concerns or employer discouragement. Employers' reluctance centers on cost and, for key employees, potential
disruption to business operations. Employees' reluctance
comes from fear that taking a leave will somehow mark
them as less committed than those who don't interrupt
their work. One manager in the media industry said that
her company had made an apparently generous offer of
an eight-week paid sabbatical every few years. But, she
added, she knew of not a single person who had taken
advantage of the benefit. It was universally assumed
that when you returned, you'd find your desk out in the
hall. You might not be fired, exactly, but the general

opinion was that you'd be displaced. This perception is unfortunate because people tend to return from sabbaticals more committed than ever. They've had a chance to recharge, to do something different, and they're appreciative of their companies for giving them the opportunity.

There are organizations that get it—that know that the cost of replacing a middlescent worker in need of a break may far outweigh the cost of the paid time off. Intel employees are eligible for an eight-week sabbatical, with full pay, after every seven years of full-time service. Silicon Graphics' regular full-time employees in the United States and Canada can take six weeks paid time off after four years. Adobe Systems offers three paid weeks off after every five years of service. Arrow Electronics offers up to ten weeks after seven years.

Hallmark Cards uses sabbaticals not only to get people out of the routine of work but also to place them into enlightening settings with the goal of recharging their artistic talent. They might spend time at the company's innovation center; go on "creative research travel" to museums, conferences, inspiring locales, or places where they can study customers and social trends; or simply spend time at the company's 172-acre farm. Most Hallmark sabbaticals are brief, but senior creative staff can also be honored with a sabbatical award of six months away from work to pursue an area of artistic exploration.

Wells Fargo's Volunteer Leave program, more than 20 years in operation, offers employees with at least five years' service and a qualifying performance rating the opportunity to work in a community service setting of their choosing for up to four months in a calendar year while receiving full pay and benefits. The work they do is often inspiring: People have used the time to volunteer at a camp for cancer victims; to represent Mothers Against Drunk Driving, traveling across the country to speak with high school students; and to work in Armenia to help women develop small businesses. This last was so successful that the project was adopted by the United Nations, and the participant was allowed to extend her leave to assist the UN in setting it up. For its part, the company reaps benefits on several fronts, including good publicity both within the corporation and out in the communities where participants are serving. The most important benefit, of course, is a returning employee who is highly energized and recommitted to the organization.

EXPANDING LEADERSHIP DEVELOPMENT

Many of the executives we spoke with in our research cited shortages in their leadership succession pipelines. On the face of it, this is surprising because, in terms of raw numbers, there are plenty of midcareer workers eager to move up the ladder and fill senior management slots. But corporate restructuring and flattening organizations have eroded the old career paths, and people can't accumulate the needed set of leadership skills on the job. The situation is sadly ironic—midcareer managers are frustrated by the lack of promotion opportunities, and corporate executives are concerned with a lack of candidates with the right experience. The solution is to widen access to leadership development programs to both rejuvenate midcareer managers and refill the leadership pipeline.

Participation in leadership development programs is a form of recognition of an employee's value and potential, and workers graduate from them with a renewed commitment to the organization's goals. But in many companies, it's difficult for people not already recognized as high potentials to get in line for these opportunities. We strongly recommend admitting late bloomers, making it easier for midcareer employees to take advantage of these programs.

Independence Blue Cross has put one-third of its top 600 people, most of them midcareer employees, through a leadership program focused on individual development and learning by doing. It includes a weeklong session at the Wharton School, individual coaching and career development planning, and work on an important business project. The insurer is now thinking about creating a graduate course for people who have already been through the program. The company is also trying to maintain career momentum after the program through a broader-based approach to succession planning and by finding its graduates new assignments that enable them to move around the business more.

The fast track should have both off- and on-ramps. A communications company shared the story of one individual who dropped off and then rejoined his company's fast track. A 12-year veteran, he had come up through finance, been deemed a high potential, and then plateaued and started to look elsewhere. Top managers at first figured, "Oh well, he wasn't CFO material anyway." But later they took a look at people who had dropped out of the high-potential program to find out why. This employee had stalled in his career because he hadn't found work that really excited him. After further assessment, he became procurement director for a product line, where his innate skills and enthusiasm as a negotiator, financial analyst, and savvy gambler paid off. In his first year, he saved the company $20 million doing work he loves.

Rekindle Now

We're not talking about rescuing a few stragglers at the corporation's fringe; we're talking about tens of millions of capable midcareer employees who are frustrated in their desire to do something new and exciting, who are stymied in their wish to contribute to the organization's success in different ways. What's stopping companies from tapping into all that potential? Perhaps it's the assumption that careers belong to employees—that people are ultimately responsible for developing their own skills, for marketing themselves, and for charting their own paths. This is true; the responsibility for career moves belongs primarily to the individual, and most employees would agree. But the fact is, organizations create the conditions under which career initiatives flourish or fade. It's in the enlightened self-interest of the organization to remove the institutional barriers to individual fulfillment and ambition, to pay the attention and devote the resources needed to keep new possibilities open and revitalize careers. This isn't paternalism—or a return to employment practices of yesterday. It's good management.

Over the next ten years, workforce demographics will turn against employers. If your organization wants to control its fate (and costs) when the boomer retirement wave and associated brain drain hit with full force, start today to systematically retain—and recruit—people with the skills and capabilities you will want to keep on hand for the long run. Recognize that many of your midcareer employees are in middlescence: For personal and professional reasons, they're getting restless. Don't just assume they'll stay, and then hope for the best. Reengage them by energizing their careers now.

The techniques we've recommended are not exclusively for midcareer workers, of course, but they will have the greatest impact on this cohort. They should prove neither expensive nor difficult to practice, and the payback—renewed commitment and productivity on the one hand, reduced replacement cost on the other—hits right away. The actions we recommend are largely a matter of paying closer attention to the often silent majority—the midcareer employees who form the heart and backbone of your workforce.

Sources of Frustration

Career Bottleneck

The baby boom generation is large, and too many people are competing for too few leadership positions in organizations that have been shedding layers of hierarchy. Next to job security, this is one of the biggest concerns of managers in their forties and fifties.

Work/Life Tension

Midcareer workers are sandwiched between commitments to children and parents, often at the same time that their work responsibilities are peaking.

Lengthening Horizon

Those who are not accumulating sufficient wealth for retirement face the prospect of having to work many more years. Many of today's midcareer employees have been lavish spenders and sparse savers.

Skills Obsolescence

Some struggle to adjust to new ways of working and managing in the information economy. Some hope that merely time or diligence will get them promoted into better and higher-paying jobs when what they most need is upgraded skills.

Disillusionment with Employer

This includes insecurity and distrust following waves of downsizing, as well as resentment over the enormous compensation gaps between topmost executives and almost all other employees.

Burnout

People who have been career driven for 20 or more years are stretched and stressed, find their work unexciting or repetitive, and are running low on energy and the ability to cope.

Career Disappointment

The roles employees play and the impact of their work fail to measure up to their youthful ideals and ambitions.

Avoiding Midcareer Crisis

TO UNDERSTAND and encourage career rejuvenation for your organization's midcareer workers, answer these ten questions:

1. Who are your keepers? Besides those on the leadership track, who has the skills, experiences, attitude, and adaptability you need most for the long term?

2. How many of your midcareer employees need to rejuvenate some of their skills or careers?

3. Are you employing any methods to rejuvenate midcareer workers? Which work best?

4. How freely does experience, knowledge, and talent flow in your company? Can employees move around the organization? What's clogging the arteries?

5. How consistently do you make each job assignment work not only for overall business performance but also for individual employee growth?

6. Do you tap people for fresh assignments when their personal circumstances change (for example, when their children grow up and leave home)?

7. Do you encourage employees to change careers within your organization?

8. Do you offer sabbaticals?

9. How often do you hire midcareer people, including workforce reentrants?

10. Do you know which jobs are particularly suited to midcareer candidates? For which jobs do you avoid hiring or assigning them? What implicit biases are holding you back?

Originally published in March 2006
Reprint R0603E

Off-Ramps and On-Ramps

*Keeping Talented Women on
the Road to Success*

SYLVIA ANN HEWLETT AND
CAROLYN BUCK LUCE

Executive Summary

MOST PROFESSIONAL WOMEN step off the career fast track at some point. With children to raise, elderly parents to care for, and other pulls on their time, these women are confronted with one off-ramp after another. When they feel pushed at the same time by long hours and unsatisfying work, the decision to leave becomes even easier. But woe to the woman who intends for that exit to be temporary. The on-ramps for professional women to get back on track are few and far between, the authors confirm. Their new survey research reveals for the first time the extent of the problem—what percentage of highly qualified women leave work and for how long, what obstacles they face coming back, and what price they pay for their time-outs.

And what are the implications for corporate America? One thing at least seems clear: As market and economic

factors align in ways guaranteed to make talent constraints and skill shortages huge issues again, employers
must learn to reverse this brain drain. Like it or not, large
numbers of highly qualified, committed women need to
take time out of the workplace. The trick is to help them
maintain connections that will allow them to reenter the
workforce without being marginalized for the rest of their
lives.

Strategies for building such connections include creating reduced-hour jobs, providing flexibility in the workday
and in the arc of a career, removing the stigma of taking
time off, refusing to burn bridges, offering outlets for altruism, and nurturing women's ambition. An HBR Special
Report, available online at www.womenscareersreport
.hbr.org, presents detailed findings of the survey.

THROUGHOUT THE PAST YEAR, a noisy debate has
erupted in the media over the meaning of what Lisa
Belkin of the *New York Times* has called the "opt-out rev-
olution." Recent articles in the *Wall Street Journal,* the
New York Times, Time, and *Fast Company* all point to a
disturbing trend—large numbers of highly qualified
women dropping out of mainstream careers. These articles also speculate on what might be behind this new
brain drain. Are the complex demands of modern child
rearing the nub of the problem? Or should one blame the
trend on a failure of female ambition?

The facts and figures in these articles are eye-
catching: a survey of the class of 1981 at Stanford University showing that 57% of women graduates leave the
work force; a survey of three graduating classes at Harvard Business School demonstrating that only 38% of
women graduates end up in full-time careers; and a

broader-gauged study of MBAs showing that one in three white women holding an MBA is not working full-time, compared with one in 20 for men with the same degree.

The stories that enliven these articles are also powerful: Brenda Barnes, the former CEO of PepsiCo, who gave up her megawatt career to spend more time with her three children; Karen Hughes, who resigned from her enormously influential job in the Bush White House to go home to Texas to better look after a needy teenage son; and a raft of less prominent women who also said goodbye to their careers. Lisa Beattie Frelinghuysen, for example—featured in a recent *60 Minutes* segment—was building a very successful career as a lawyer. She'd been president of the law review at Stanford and went to work for a prestigious law firm. She quit after she had her first baby three years later.

These stories certainly resonate, but scratch the surface and it quickly becomes clear that there is very little in the way of systematic, rigorous data about the seeming exodus. A sector here, a graduating class there, and a flood of anecdotes: No one seems to know the basic facts. Across professions and across sectors, what is the scope of this opt-out phenomenon? What proportion of professional women take off-ramps rather than continue on their chosen career paths? Are they pushed off or pulled? Which sectors of the economy are most severely affected when women leave the workforce? How many years do women tend to spend out of the workforce? When women decide to reenter, what are they looking for? How easy is it to find on-ramps? What policies and practices help women return to work?

Early in 2004, the Center for Work-Life Policy formed a private sector, multiyear task force entitled "The Hidden Brain Drain: Women and Minorities as Unrealized

Assets" to answer these and other questions. In the summer of 2004, three member companies of the task force (Ernst & Young, Goldman Sachs, and Lehman Brothers) sponsored a survey specifically designed to investigate the role of off-ramps and on-ramps in the lives of highly qualified women. The survey, conducted by Harris Interactive, comprised a nationally representative group of highly qualified women, defined as those with a graduate degree, a professional degree, or a high-honors undergraduate degree. The sample size was 2,443 women. The survey focused on two age groups: older women aged 41 to 55 and younger women aged 28 to 40. We also surveyed a smaller group of highly qualified men (653) to allow us to draw comparisons.

Using the data from the survey, we've created a more comprehensive and nuanced portrait of women's career paths than has been available to date. Even more important, these data suggest actions that companies can take to ensure that female potential does not go unrealized. Given current demographic and labor market trends, it's imperative that employers learn to reverse this brain drain. Indeed, companies that can develop policies and practices to tap into the female talent pool over the long haul will enjoy a substantial competitive advantage.

Women Do Leave

Many women take an off-ramp at some point on their career highway. Nearly four in ten highly qualified women (37%) report that they have left work voluntarily at some point in their careers. Among women who have children, that statistic rises to 43%. (See the exhibit "How Many Opt Out?")

Factors other than having children that pull women away from their jobs include the demands of caring for elderly parents or other family members (reported by 24%) and personal health issues (9%). Not surprisingly, the pull of elder care responsibilities is particularly strong for women in the 41 to 55 age group—often called the "sandwich" generation, positioned as it is between growing children and aging parents. One in three women in that bracket have left work for some period to spend time caring for family members who are not children. And lurking behind all this is the pervasiveness of a highly traditional division of labor on the home front. In a 2001 survey conducted by the Center for Work-Life Policy, fully 40% of highly qualified women with spouses felt that their husbands create more work around the house than they perform.

Alongside these "pull" factors are a series of "push" factors—that is, features of the job or workplace that make women head for the door. Seventeen percent of

How Many Opt Out?

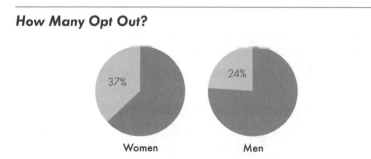

In our survey of highly qualified professionals, we asked the question, "Since you first began working, has there ever been a period where you took a voluntary time out from work?" Nearly four in ten women reported that they had—and that statistic rises to 43% among women who have children. By contrast, only 24% of highly qualified men have taken off-ramps (with no statistical difference between those who are fathers and those who are not).

women say they took an off-ramp, at least in part, because their jobs were not satisfying or meaningful. Overall, understimulation and lack of opportunity seem to be larger problems than overwork. Only 6% of women stopped working because the work itself was too demanding. In business sectors, the survey results suggest that push factors are particularly powerful—indeed, in these sectors, unlike, say, in medicine or teaching, they outweigh pull factors. Of course, in the hurly-burly world of everyday life, most women are dealing with a combination of push and pull factors—and one often serves to intensify the other. When women feel hemmed in by rigid policies or a glass ceiling, for example, they are much more likely to respond to the pull of family.

It's important to note that, however pulled or pushed, only a relatively privileged group of women have the option of not working. Most women cannot quit their careers unless their spouses earn considerable incomes. Fully 32% of the women surveyed cite the fact that their spouses' income "was sufficient for our family to live on one income" as a reason contributing to their decision to off-ramp.

Contrast this with the experience of highly qualified men, only 24% of whom have taken off-ramps (with no statistical difference between those who are fathers and those who are not). When men leave the workforce, they do it for different reasons. Child-care and elder-care responsibilities are much less important; only 12% of men cite these factors as compared with 44% of women. Instead, on the pull side, they cite switching careers (29%), obtaining additional training (25%), or starting a business (12%) as important reasons for taking time out. For highly qualified men, off-ramping seems to be about strategic repositioning in their careers—a far cry from the dominant concerns of their female peers. (See the exhibit "Why Do They Leave the Fast Lane?")

For many women in our study, the decision to off-ramp is a tough one. These women have invested heavily in their education and training. They have spent years accumulating the skills and credentials necessary for successful careers. Most are not eager to toss that painstaking effort aside.

Why Do They Leave the Fast Lane?

Our survey data show that women and men take off-ramps for dramatically different reasons. While men leave the workforce mainly to reposition themselves for a career change, the majority of women off-ramp to attend to responsibilities at home.

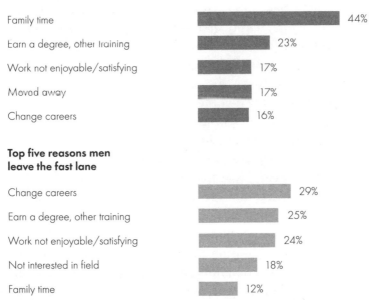

Top five reasons women leave the fast lane

Family time	44%
Earn a degree, other training	23%
Work not enjoyable/satisfying	17%
Moved away	17%
Change careers	16%

Top five reasons men leave the fast lane

Change careers	29%
Earn a degree, other training	25%
Work not enjoyable/satisfying	24%
Not interested in field	18%
Family time	12%

Lost on Reentry

Among women who take off-ramps, the overwhelming majority have every intention of returning to the work-force—and seemingly little idea of just how difficult that will prove. Women, like lawyer Lisa Beattie Freling-huysen from the *60 Minutes* segment, who happily give up their careers to have children are the exception rather than the rule. In our research, we find that most highly qualified women who are currently off-ramped (93%) want to return to their careers.

Many of these women have financial reasons for wanting to get back to work. Nearly half (46%) cite "hav-ing their own independent source of income" as an important propelling factor. Women who participated in focus groups conducted as part of our research talked about their discomfort with "dependence." However good their marriages, many disliked needing to ask for money. Not being able to splurge on some small extrava-gance or make their own philanthropic choices without clearing it with their husbands did not sit well with them. It's also true that a significant proportion of women currently seeking on-ramps are facing troubling shortfalls in family income: 38% cite "household income no longer sufficient for family needs" and 24% cite "part-ner's income no longer sufficient for family needs." Given what has happened to the cost of homes (up 38% over the past five years), the cost of college education (up 40% over the past decade), and the cost of health insurance (up 49% since 2000), it's easy to see why many profes-sional families find it hard to manage on one income.

But financial pressure does not tell the whole story. Many of these women find deep pleasure in their chosen careers and want to reconnect with something they love.

Forty-three percent cite the "enjoyment and satisfaction" they derive from their careers as an important reason to return—among teachers this figure rises to 54% and among doctors it rises to 70%. A further 16% want to "regain power and status in their profession." In our focus groups, women talked eloquently about how work gives shape and structure to their lives, boosts confidence and self-esteem, and confers status and standing in their communities. For many off-rampers, their professional identities remain their primary identities, despite the fact that they have taken time out.

Perhaps most interesting, 24% of the women currently looking for on-ramps are motivated by "a desire to give something back to society" and are seeking jobs that allow them to contribute to their communities in some way. In our focus groups, off-ramped women talked about how their time at home had changed their aspirations. Whether they had gotten involved in protecting the wetlands, supporting the local library, or rebuilding a playground, they felt newly connected to the importance of what one woman called "the work of care."

Unfortunately, only 74% of off-ramped women who want to rejoin the ranks of the employed manage to do so, according to our survey. And among these, only 40% return to full-time, professional jobs. Many (24%) take part-time jobs, and some (9%) become self-employed. The implication is clear: Off-ramps are around every curve in the road, but once a woman has taken one, on-ramps are few and far between—and extremely costly.

The Penalties of Time Out

Women off-ramp for surprisingly short periods of time—on average, 2.2 years. In business sectors, off-rampers average even shorter periods of time out (1.2 years). However, even these relatively short career interruptions entail heavy financial penalties. Our data show that women lose an average of 18% of their earning power when they take an off-ramp. In business sectors, penalties are particularly draconian: In these fields, women's earning power dips an average of 28% when they take time out. The longer you spend out, the more severe the penalty becomes. Across sectors, women lose a staggering 37% of their earning power when they spend three or more years out of the workforce. (See the exhibit "The High Cost of Time Out.")

The High Cost of Time Out

Though the average amount of time that women take off from their careers is surprisingly short (less than three years), the salary penalty for doing so is severe. Women who return to the workforce after time out earn significantly less than their peers who remained in their jobs.

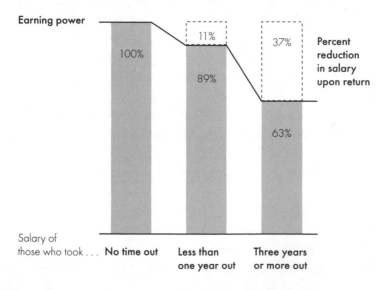

Naomi, 34, is a case in point. In an interview, this part-time working mother was open about her anxieties: "Every day, I think about what I am going to do when I want to return to work full-time. I worry about whether I will be employable—will anyone even look at my résumé?" This is despite an MBA and substantial work experience.

Three years ago, Naomi felt she had no choice but to quit her lucrative position in market research. She had just had a child, and returning to full-time work after the standard maternity leave proved to be well-nigh impossible. Her 55-hour week combined with her husband's 80-hour week didn't leave enough time to raise a healthy child—let alone care for a child who was prone to illness, as theirs was. When her employer denied her request to work reduced hours, Naomi quit.

After nine months at home, Naomi did find some flexible work—but it came at a high price. Her new freelance job as a consultant to an advertising agency barely covered the cost of her son's day care. She now earns a third of what she did three years ago. What plagues Naomi the most about her situation is her anxiety about the future. "Will my skills become obsolete? Will I be able to support myself and my son if something should happen to my husband?"

The scholarly literature shows that Naomi's experience is not unusual. Economist Jane Waldfogel has analyzed the pattern of earnings over the life span. When women enter the workforce in their early and mid twenties they earn nearly as much as men do. For a few years, they almost keep pace. For example, at ages 25 to 29, they earn 87% of the male wage. However, when women start having children, their earnings fall way behind those of men. By the time they reach the 40-to-44 age group, women earn a mere 71% of the male wage. In the words of MIT economist Lester Thurow, "These are the prime years for establishing a successful career. These are the years when hard work has the maximum payoff. They are also the prime years for launching a family. Women who leave the job market during those years may find that they never catch up."

Taking the Scenic Route

A majority (58%) of highly qualified women describe their careers as "nonlinear"—which is to say, they do not follow the conventional trajectory long established by successful men. That ladder of success features a steep gradient in one's 30s and steady progress thereafter. In contrast, these women report that their "career paths have not followed a progression through the hierarchy of an industry."

Some of this nonlinearity is the result of taking off-ramps. But there are many other ways in which women ease out of the professional fast lane. Our survey reveals that 16% of highly qualified women work part-time. Such arrangements are more prevalent in the legal and medical professions, where 23% and 20% of female professionals work less than full-time, than in the business sector, where only 8% of women work part-time. Another common work-life strategy is telecommuting; 8% of highly qualified women work exclusively from home, and another 25% work partly from home.

Looking back over their careers, 36% of highly qualified women say they have worked part-time for some period of time as part of a strategy to balance work and personal life. Twenty-five percent say they have reduced the number of work hours within a full-time job, and

16% say they have declined a promotion. A significant proportion (38%) say they have deliberately chosen a position with fewer responsibilities and lower compensation than they were qualified for, in order to fulfill responsibilities at home.

Downsizing Ambition

Given the tour of women's careers we've just taken, is it any surprise that women find it difficult to claim or sustain ambition? The survey shows that while almost half of the men consider themselves extremely or very ambitious, only about a third of the women do. (The proportion rises among women in business and the professions of law and medicine; there, 43% and 51%, respectively, consider themselves very ambitious.) In a similar vein, only 15% of highly qualified women (and 27% in the business sector) single out "a powerful position" as an important career goal; in fact, this goal ranked lowest in women's priorities in every sector we surveyed.

Far more important to these women are other items on the workplace wish list: the ability to associate with people they respect (82%); the freedom to "be themselves" at work (79%); and the opportunity to be flexible with their schedules (64%). Fully 61% of women consider it extremely or very important to have the opportunity to collaborate with others and work as part of a team. A majority (56%) believe it is very important for them to be able to give back to the community through their work. And 51% find "recognition from my company" either extremely or very important.

These top priorities constitute a departure from the traditional male take on ambition. Moreover, further analysis points to a disturbing age gap. In the business sector, 53% of younger women (ages 28 to 40) own up to being very ambitious, as contrasted with only 37% of older women. This makes sense in light of Anna Fels's groundbreaking work on women and ambition. In a 2004 HBR article, Fels argues convincingly that ambition stands on two legs—mastery and recognition. To hold onto their dreams, not only must women attain the necessary skills and experience, they must also have their achievements appropriately recognized. To the extent the latter is missing in female careers, ambition is undermined. A vicious cycle emerges: As women's ambitions stall, they are perceived as less committed, they no longer get the best assignments, and this lowers their ambitions further.

In our focus groups, we heard the disappointment—and discouragement—of women who had reached senior levels in corporations only to find the glass ceiling still in place, despite years of diversity initiatives. These women feel that they are languishing and have not been given either the opportunities or the recognition that would allow them to realize their full potential. Many feel handicapped in the attainment of their goals. The result is the vicious cycle that Fels describes: a "downsizing" of women's ambition that becomes a self-fulfilling prophecy. And the discrepancy in ambition levels between men and women has an insidious side effect in that it results in insufficient role models for younger women.

Reversing the Brain Drain

These, then, are the hard facts. With them in hand, we move from anecdotes to data—and, more important, to a different, richer analytical understanding of the problem. In the structural issue of off-ramps and on-ramps, we see the mechanism derailing the careers of highly qualified women and also the focal point for making positive change. What are the implications for corporate America? One thing at least seems clear: Employers can no longer pretend that treating women as "men in skirts" will fix their retention problems. Like it or not, large numbers of highly qualified, committed women need to take time out. The trick is to help them maintain connections that will allow them to come back from that time without being marginalized for the rest of their careers. (See the insert "How Ernst & Young Keeps Women on the Path to Partnership" at the end of this article.)

Create reduced-hour jobs.   The most obvious way to stay connected is to offer women with demanding lives a way to keep a hand in their chosen field, short of full-time involvement. Our survey found that, in business sectors, fully 89% of women believe that access to reduced-hour jobs is important. Across all sectors, the figure is 82%.

The Johnson & Johnson family of companies has seen the increased loyalty and productivity that can result from such arrangements. We recently held a focus group with 12 part-time managers at these companies and found a level of commitment that was palpable. The women had logged histories with J&J that ranged from eight to 19 years and spoke of the corporation with great affection. All had a focus on productivity and pushed themselves to deliver at the same level they had achieved before switching to part-time. One woman, a 15-year J&J veteran, was particularly eloquent in her gratitude to the corporation. She had had her first child at age 40 and, like so many new mothers, felt torn apart by the conflicting demands of home and work. In her words, "I thought I only had two choices—work full-time or leave—and I didn't want either. J&J's reduced-hour option has been a savior." All the women in the room were clear on one point: They would have quit had part-time jobs not been available.

At Pfizer, the deal is sweetened further for part-time workers; field sales professionals in the company's Vista Rx division are given access to the same benefits and training as full-time employees but work 60% of the hours (with a corresponding difference in base pay). Many opt for a three-day workweek; others structure their working day around children's school hours. These 230 employees—93% of whom are working mothers—remain eligible for promotion and may return to full-time status at their discretion.

Provide flexibility in the day. Some women don't require reduced work hours; they merely need flexibility in when, where, and how they do their work. Even parents who employ nannies or have children in day care, for example, must make time for teacher conferences, medical appointments, volunteering, child-related errands—not to mention the days the nanny calls in sick or the day care center is closed. Someone caring for an invalid or a fragile elderly person may likewise have many hours of potentially productive time in a day yet not be able to stray far from home.

For these and other reasons, almost two-thirds (64%) of the women we surveyed cite flexible work arrangements as being either extremely or very important to them. In fact, by a considerable margin, highly qualified women find flexibility more important than compensation; only 42% say that "earning a lot of money" is an important motivator. In our focus groups, we heard women use terms like "nirvana" and "the golden ring" to describe employment arrangements that allow them to flex their workdays, their workweeks, and their careers. A senior employee who recently joined Lehman Brothers' equity division is an example. She had been working at another financial services company when a Lehman recruiter called. "The person who had been in the job previously was working one day a week from home, so they offered that opportunity to me. Though I was content in my current job," she told us, "that intriguing possibility made me reevaluate. In the end, I took the job at Lehman. Working from home one day a week was a huge lure."

Provide flexibility in the arc of a career. Booz Allen Hamilton, the management and technology consulting firm, recognized that it isn't simply a workday, or a workweek, that needs to be made more flexible. It's the entire arc of a career.

Management consulting as a profession loses twice as many women as men in the middle reaches of career ladders. A big part of the problem is that, perhaps more than in any other business sector, it is driven by an up-or-out ethos; client-serving professionals must progress steadily or fall by the wayside. The strongest contenders make partner through a relentless winnowing process. While many firms take care to make the separations as painless as possible (the chaff, after all, tends to land in organizations that might employ their services), there are clear limits to their patience. Typically, if a valued professional is unable to keep pace with the road warrior lifestyle, the best she can hope for is reassignment to a staff job.

Over the past year, Booz Allen has initiated a "ramp up, ramp down" flexible program to allow professionals to balance work and life and still do the client work they find most interesting. The key to the program is Booz Allen's effort to "unbundle" standard consulting projects and identify chunks that can be done by telecommuting or shorts stints in the office. Participating professionals are either regular employees or alumni that sign standard employment contracts and are activated as needed. For the professional, it's a way to take on a manageable amount of the kind of work they do best. For Booz Allen, it's a way to maintain ties to consultants who have already proved their merit in a challenging profession. Since many of these talented women will eventually return to full-time consulting employment, Booz Allen wants to be their employer of choice—and to keep their skills sharp in the meantime.

When asked how the program is being received, DeAnne Aguirre, a vice president at Booz Allen who was involved in its design (and who is also a member of our task force), had an instant reaction: "I think it's instilled new hope—a lot of young women I work with no longer feel that they will have to sacrifice some precious part of themselves." Aguirre explains that trade-offs are inevitable, but at Booz Allen an off-ramping decision doesn't have to be a devastating one anymore. "Flex careers are bound to be slower than conventional ones, but in ten years' time you probably won't remember the precise year you made partner. The point here is to remain on track and vitally connected."

Remove the stigma. Making flexible arrangements succeed over the long term is hard work. It means crafting an imaginative set of policies, but even more important, it means eliminating the stigma that is often attached to such nonstandard work arrangements. As many as 35% of the women we surveyed report various aspects of their organizations' cultures that effectively penalize people who take advantage of work-life policies. Telecommuting appears to be most stigmatized, with 39% of women reporting some form of tacit resistance to it, followed by job sharing and part-time work. Of flexible work arrangements in general, 21% report that "there is an unspoken rule at my workplace that people who use these options will not be promoted." Parental leave policies get more respect—though even here, 19% of women report cultural or attitudinal barriers to taking the time off that they are entitled to. In environments where flexible work arrangements are tacitly deemed illegitimate, many women would rather resign than request them.

Interestingly, when it comes to taking advantage of work-life policies, men encounter even more stigma. For example, 48% of the men we surveyed perceived job sharing as illegitimate in their workplace culture—even when it's part of official policy.

Transformation of the corporate culture seems to be a prerequisite for success on the work-life front. Those people at or near the top of an organization need to have that "eureka" moment, when they not only understand the business imperative for imaginative work-life policies but are prepared to embrace them, and in so doing remove the stigma. In the words of Dessa Bokides, treasurer at Pitney Bowes, "Only a leader's devotion to these issues will give others permission to transform conventional career paths."

Stop burning bridges. One particularly dramatic finding of our survey deserves special mention: Only 5% of highly qualified women looking for on-ramps are interested in rejoining the companies they left. In business sectors, that percentage is zero. If ever there was a danger signal for corporations, this is it.

The finding implies that the vast majority of off-ramped women, at the moment they left their careers, felt ill-used—or at least underutilized and unappreciated—by their employers. We can only speculate as to why this was. In some cases, perhaps, the situation ended badly; a woman, attempting impossible juggling feats, started dropping balls. Or an employer, embittered by the loss of too many "star" women, lets this one go much too easily.

It's understandable for managers to assume that women leave mainly for "pull" reasons and that there's no point in trying to keep them. Indeed, when family overload and the traditional division of labor place unmanageable demands on a working woman, it does appear that quitting has much more to do with what's going on at home than what's going on at work. However, it is important to realize that even when pull factors seem to be dominant, push factors are also in play. Most off-ramping decisions are conditioned by policies, practices, and attitudes at work. Recognition, flexibility, and the opportunity to telecommute—especially when endorsed by the corporate culture—can make a huge difference.

The point is, managers will not stay in a departing employee's good graces unless they take the time to explore the reasons for off-ramping and are able and willing to offer options short of total severance. If a company wants future access to this talent, it will need to go beyond the perfunctory exit interview and, at the very least, impart the message that the door is open. Better

still, it will maintain a connection with off-ramped
employees through a formal alumni program.

Provide outlets for altruism. Imaginative attachment
policies notwithstanding, some women have no interest
in returning to their old organizations because their
desire to work in their former field has waned. Recall the
focus group participants who spoke of a deepened desire
to give back to the community after taking a hiatus from
work. Remember, too, that women in business sectors
are pushed off track more by dissatisfaction with work
than pulled by external demands. Our data suggest that
fully 52% of women with MBAs in the business sector
cite the fact that they do not find their careers "either
satisfying or enjoyable" as an important reason for why
they left work. Perhaps not surprisingly, then, a majority
(54%) of the women looking for on-ramps want to
change their profession or field. And in most of those
cases, it's a woman who formerly worked in the corporate sphere hoping to move into the not-for-profit sector.

Employers would be well advised to recognize and
harness the altruism of these women. Supporting female
professionals in their advocacy and public service efforts
serves to win their energy and loyalty. Companies may
also be able to redirect women's desire to give back to
the community by asking them to become involved in
mentoring and formal women's networks within the
company.

Nurture ambition. Finally, if women are to sustain
their passion for work and their competitive edge—
whether or not they take formal time out—they must
keep ambition alive. Our findings point to an urgent need
to implement mentoring and networking programs that

help women expand and sustain their professional aspirations. Companies like American Express, GE, Goldman Sachs, Johnson & Johnson, Lehman Brothers, and Time Warner are developing "old girls networks" that build skills, contacts, and confidence. They link women to inside power brokers and to outside business players and effectively inculcate those precious rainmaking skills.

Networks (with fund-raising and friend-raising functions) can enhance client connections. But they also play another, critical role. They provide the infrastructure within which women can earn recognition, as well as a safe platform from which to blow one's own horn without being perceived as too pushy. In the words of Patricia Fili-Krushel, executive vice president of Time Warner, "Company-sponsored women's networks encourage women to cultivate both sides of the power equation. Women hone their own leadership abilities but also learn to use power on behalf of others. Both skill sets help us increase our pipeline of talented women."

Adopt an On-Ramp

As we write this, market and economic factors, both cyclical and structural, are aligned in ways guaranteed to make talent constraints and skill shortages huge issues again. Unemployment is down and labor markets are beginning to tighten, just as the baby-bust generation is about to hit "prime time" and the number of workers between the ages of 35 to 45 is shrinking. Immigration levels are stable, so there's little chance of relief there. Likewise, productivity improvements are flattening. The phenomenon that bailed us out of our last big labor crunch—the entry for the first time of millions of women into the labor force—is not available to us again. Add it all up, and CEOs are back to wondering how they will find enough high-caliber talent to drive growth.

There is a winning strategy. It revolves around the retention and reattachment of highly qualified women. America these days has a large and impressive pool of female talent. Fifty-eight percent of college graduates are now women, and nearly half of all professional and graduate degrees are earned by women. Even more important, the incremental additions to the talent pool will be disproportionately female, according to figures released by the U.S. Department of Education. The number of women with graduate and professional degrees is projected to grow by 16% over the next decade, while the number of men with these degrees is projected to grow by a mere 1.3%. Companies are beginning to pay attention to these figures. As Melinda Wolfe, head of global leadership and diversity at Goldman Sachs, recently pointed out, "A large part of the potential talent pool consists of females and historically underrepresented groups. With the professional labor market tightening, it is in our direct interest to give serious attention to these matters of retention and reattachment."

In short, the talent is there; the challenge is to create the circumstances that allow businesses to take advantage of it over the long run. To tap this all-important resource, companies must understand the complexities of women's nonlinear careers and be prepared to support rather than punish those who take alternate routes.

The complete statistical findings from this research project, and additional commentary and company examples, are available in an HBR research report entitled "The Hidden Brain Drain: Off-Ramps and On-Ramps in Women's Careers" (see www.womenscareersreport.hbr.org).

How Ernst & Young Keeps Women on the Path to Partnership

IN THE MID-1990S, turnover among female employees at Ernst & Young was much higher than it was among male peers. Company leaders knew something was seriously wrong; for many years, its entering classes of young auditors had been made up of nearly equal numbers of men and women—yet it was still the case that only a tiny percentage of its partnership was female. This was a major problem. Turnover in client-serving roles meant lost continuity on work assignments. And on top of losing talent that the firm had invested in training, E&Y was incurring costs averaging 150% of a departing employee's annual salary just to fill the vacant position.

E&Y set a new course, marked by several important features outlined here. Since E&Y began this work, the percentage of women partners has more than tripled to 12% and the downward trend in retention of women at every level has been reversed. E&Y now has four women on the management board, and many more women are in key operating and client serving roles. Among its women partners, 10% work on a flexible schedule and more than 20 have been promoted to partner while working a reduced schedule. In 2004, 22% of new partners were women.

Focus

Regional pilot projects targeted five areas for improvement: Palo Alto and San Jose focused on life balance, Minneapolis on mentoring, New Jersey on flexible work arrangements, Boston on women networking in the business community, and Washington, DC, on women networking inside E&Y. Successful solutions were rolled out across the firm.

Committed Leadership

Philip Laskawy, E&Y's chairman from 1994 to 2001, made it a priority to retain and promote women. He convened a diversity task force of partners to focus on the problem and created an Office of Retention. Laskawy's successor, Jim Turley, deepened the focus on diversity by rolling out a People First strategy.

Policies

Ernst & Young equipped all its people for telework and made it policy that flexible work schedules would not affect anyone's opportunity for advancement. The new premise was that all jobs could be done flexibly.

New Roles

E&Y's Center for the New Workforce dedicates its staff of seven to developing and advancing women into leadership roles. A strategy team of three professionals addresses the firm's flexibility goals for both men and women. Also, certain partners are designated as "career watchers" and track individual women's progress, in particular, monitoring the caliber of the projects and clients to which they are assigned.

Learning Resources

All employees can use E&Y's Achieving Flexibility Web site to learn about flexible work arrangements. They can track how certain FWAs were negotiated and structured and can use the contact information provided in the database to ask those employees questions about how it is (or isn't) working.

Peer Networking

Professional Women's Networks are active in 41 offices, and they focus on building the skills, confidence, leadership opportunities, and networks necessary for women to be successful. A three-day Women's Leadership Conference is held every 18 months. The most recent was attended by more than 425 women partners, principals, and directors.

Accountability

The annual People Point survey allows employees to rate managers on how well they foster an inclusive, flexible work environment. Managers are also evaluated on metrics like number of women serving key accounts, in key leadership jobs, and in the partner pipeline.

Originally published in March 2005
Reprint R0503B

It's Time to Retire Retirement

KEN DYCHTWALD, TAMARA J. ERICKSON,
AND ROBERT MORISON

Executive Summary

COMPANIES HAVE BEEN SO FOCUSED on downsizing
to contain costs that they've largely neglected a looming
threat to their competitiveness: a severe shortage of talented workers. The general population is aging and with
it, the labor pool. People are living longer, healthier lives,
and the birthrate is at a historical low.

During the next 15 years, 80% of the native-born
workforce growth in North America—and even more in
much of Western Europe—is going to be in the over-50
age cohort. When these mature workers begin to retire,
there won't be nearly enough young people entering the
workforce to compensate. The Bureau of Labor Statistics
projects a shortfall of 10 million workers in the United
States in 2010, and in countries where the birthrate is
well below the population replacement level (particularly

in Western Europe), the shortage will hit sooner, be more severe, and remain chronic.

The problem won't just be a lack of bodies. Skills, knowledge, experience, and relationships walk out the door every time somebody retires—and they take time and money to replace. And while the brain drain is beginning now, the problem is going to become much more acute in the next decade or so, when baby boomers—more than one-quarter of all Americans, amounting to 76 million people—start hitting their mid sixties.

Based on the results of their yearlong research project, the authors of this article offer recommendations for gaining the loyalty of older workers and creating a more flexible approach to retirement that allows people to continue contributing well into their sixties and seventies. Companies can no longer afford to think of retirement as a onetime event, permanently dividing work life from leisure.

In the past few years, companies have been so focused on downsizing to contain costs that they've largely neglected a looming threat to their competitiveness, the likes of which they have never before experienced: a severe shortage of talented workers. The general population is aging and, with it, the labor pool. People are living longer, healthier lives, and the birthrate is at a historic low. While the ranks of the youngest workers (ages 16 to 24, according to Bureau of Labor Statistics groupings) are growing 15% this decade as baby boomers' children enter the workforce, the 25- to 34-year-old segment is growing at just half that rate, and the workforce population between the ages of 35 and 44—the prime executive-development years—is actually declining.

In the United States, the overall rate of workforce growth faces a sharp drop. After peaking at nearly 30% in the 1970s (as the baby boomers as well as unprecedented numbers of women entered the workforce), and holding relatively steady at 12% during the 1990s and again in the present decade, the rate is projected to drop and level off at 2% to 3% per decade thereafter. That translates into an annual growth rate of less than 1% today and an anemic 0.2% by 2020. Meanwhile, age distributions are shifting dramatically. The proportion of workers over 55 declined from 18% in the 1970s to under 11% in 2000—but it's projected to rebound to 20% by 2015. In other words, we've recently passed what will prove to be a historic low in the concentration of older workers. Just when we've gotten accustomed to having relatively few mature workers around, we have to start learning how to attract and retain far more of them.

During the next 15 years, 80% of the native-born workforce growth in North America—and even more so in much of Western Europe—is going to be in the over-50 cohort. In the next decade or so, when baby boomers—the 76 million people born between 1946 and 1964, more than one-quarter of all Americans—start hitting their sixties and contemplating retirement, there won't be nearly enough young people entering the workforce to compensate for the exodus. The Bureau of Labor Statistics projects a shortfall of 10 million workers in the United States in 2010, and in countries where the birthrate is well below the population replacement level (particularly in Western Europe), the shortage will hit sooner, be more severe, and remain chronic.

The problem won't just be a lack of bodies. Skills, knowledge, experience, and relationships walk out the door every time somebody retires—and they take time and money to replace. Given the inevitable time lag between the demand for skills and the ability of the educational system to provide them, we'll see a particularly pronounced skill shortage in fast-growing technical fields such as health care. What's more, employees are your face to the marketplace. It's good business to have employees who reflect the ethnic, gender, and, yes, age composition of your customer base—especially when those customers are well off. Baby boomers will be the most financially powerful generation of mature consumers ever; today's mature adults control more than $7 trillion in wealth in the United States—70% of the total. As the population at large ages, and ever-more spending power is concentrated in the hands of older customers, companies will want to show a mature face to their clientele—and yet those faces will be in high demand.

The problem is pretty clear. Workers will be harder to come by. Tacit knowledge will melt steadily away from your organization. And the most dramatic shortage of workers will hit the age group associated with leadership and key customer-facing positions. The good news is that a solution is at hand: Just as companies are learning to market to an aging population, so they can also learn to attract and employ older workers.

And yet, despite irrefutable evidence of workforce aging, many managers may be marching their companies straight off a demographic cliff. According to a recent survey from the Society for Human Resource Management, two-thirds of U.S. employers don't actively recruit older workers. Furthermore, more than half do not actively attempt to retain key ones; 80% do not offer any special provisions (such as flexible work arrangements) to appeal to the concerns of mature workers; and 60% of CEOs say their companies don't account for workforce aging in their long-term business plans. Instead, relying on the mistaken assumption that the future will be populated by a growing pool of talented and loyal young workers, companies are systemically offering older workers the "package" and skimming people out of the labor force from the top age brackets down. (See the exhibit "Who Will Run Your Company?")

Little wonder that baby boomers and "mature" workers (those 55 and above) are feeling little loyalty to their current employers. These employees are bottlenecked, with too many people competing for too few leadership positions. They're distrustful, fearful, and defensive, knowing that they're "too old" to easily find work elsewhere and likely to be pushed out before the "official" retirement age. They're struggling to update their skills, and they're feeling burned out after 30-plus years on the job. Meanwhile, they stand back and watch as recruiting, training, and leadership development dollars, as well as promotion opportunities, are overwhelmingly directed at younger employees, with little thought to the skills and experience that the over-55 crowd can bring to bear on almost any business problem.

In short, most baby boomers want to continue working—and they may need to, for financial reasons—but they may not want to work for you. Twenty percent of those collecting employer pensions are still working in some capacity, and among people under 60 who are already collecting pensions, more than 50% are working. Among those age 55 and older who accepted early retirement offers, one-third have gone back to work. But these working retirees are more likely to be working part-time

or be self-employed than their not-yet-retired counterparts—in other words, they're working on their own
terms. That's increasingly where you'll need to meet
these older workers if you want to gain access to their
skills. As the labor market tightens, they will have more

Who Will Run Your Company?

*If we look at workforce growth rates by age segment, the patterns are
dramatic. In the current decade, the ranks of youngest workers (age 16
to 24, according to Bureau of Labor Statistics groupings) are growing by
15%, thanks to the "echo boom" as baby boomers' children enter the
workforce. The 25- to 34-year-old segment is growing at just half that
rate, and the workforce population between 35 and 44 years old is
actually declining. With the baby boom generation moving into middle
age and its vanguard nearing retirement age, the fastest workforce
growth rates are in the three oldest age segments.*

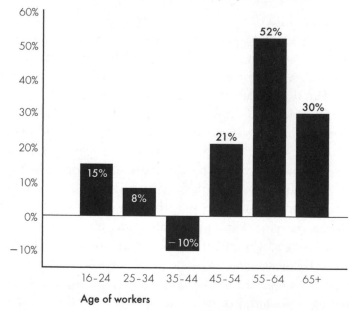

Growth in U.S. Workforce by Age, 2000–2010

choices, and the most capable and accomplished among them are likely to be the most mobile and financially independent; they're the ones who are most likely to move on. The challenge is to find a way to reconnect with these employees before they're ready to take a retirement package and run—perhaps to a competitor.

We recently conducted a yearlong research project in which we looked at the implications for businesses of an aging workforce. Broadly speaking, our findings suggest an urgent need to find ways to attract and retain employees of all ages. But of most concern is the potentially debilitating mass retirement that threatens to starve many businesses of key talent in the next ten to 15 years. On the basis of our research, we've concluded that the concept of retirement is outdated and should be put out to pasture in favor of a more flexible approach to ongoing work, one that serves both employer and employee. In this article, we'll describe how companies can retain the skills of employees well past the traditional age of retirement by moving from a rigid model where work ceases at a certain age to a more flexible one where employees can become lifelong contributors.

Create a Culture That Honors Experience

If companies are to win back the hearts and minds of baby boomers and other generations of mature workers, they need to start with the work environment itself, which has become increasingly alienating to anyone over the age of 50. Human resource practices are often explicitly or implicitly biased against older workers, and these biases can seep into the culture in a manner that makes them feel unwelcome.

It starts with recruiting, in subtle ways such as the choice of words in a job advertisement. Even high-energy, young-in-spirit older workers, for example, may interpret an ad stressing "energy," "fast pace," and "fresh thinking" as implicitly targeting younger workers and dismiss the opportunity out of hand. Mature workers are more likely to be attracted to ads emphasizing "experience," "knowledge," and "expertise."

Traditional recruiting channels such as want ads or help wanted signs may not attract older workers either. Twelve years ago, pharmacy chain CVS looked at national demographic trends and concluded that the company needed to employ a much greater number of older workers. But managers didn't know how to find them—older people shopped in the stores but didn't apply for openings, perhaps believing they wouldn't be hired. Now the company works through the National Council on Aging, city agencies, and community organizations to find and hire productive new employees.

Interviewing techniques can be unintentionally off-putting as well. Being left alone for half an hour to build something with Legos or being asked to perform the type of verbal gymnastics Microsoft became famous for in job interviews (example: how are M&Ms made?) may be daunting to candidates accustomed to a more traditional approach to demonstrating their skills. One major British bank realized that its psychometric and verbal-reasoning tests were intimidating to older candidates and replaced these tests with role-playing exercises to gauge candidates' ability to handle customers. And Nationwide, Britain's largest building society, has begun short-listing job candidates by telephone to reduce the number of applicants who are rejected because they look older.

Training and development activities also tend to favor younger employees. According to the Bureau of Labor Statistics, older workers (age 55 plus) receive on average less than half the amount of training that any of their younger cohorts receive, including workers in the 45 to 54 age range. One reason may be that they're reluctant to ask: As people well established in their careers and very busy on the job, they may not feel or want to admit the need for training and development. And yet many mid-career and older employees require refresher training in areas from information technology to functional disciplines to nonhierarchical management methods. The challenge is to make them feel as though it's not a sign of weakness to ask. At Dow Chemical, the companywide expectation is that employees at all levels will continue to learn and grow; as a result, employees regularly seek training and development opportunities, readying themselves for their next career moves.

Most important, mature workers will be attracted to a culture that values their experience and capabilities—an environment that can take some time and effort to build. The Aerospace Corporation is a company that has, over the years, built a reputation for valuing experience and knowledge. Nearly half of its 3,400 regular, full-time employees are over age 50—a clear signal to job candidates that experience is appreciated. CVS has made great strides in creating a company that is more welcoming to older employees, having more than doubled the percentage of employees over age 50 in the past 12 years. It has no mandatory retirement age, making it easy to join the company at an advanced age and stay indefinitely (six employees are in their nineties). The company boosts its age-friendly image through internal and external publications. Company and HR department newsletters highlight the productivity and effectiveness of older workers, and the company coproduces with a cosmetics company a senior-focused magazine that's called *In Step with Healthy Living*.

Older workers can see that CVS honors experience. A year ago, after taking a buyout package from his management job in a major drugstore chain, 59-year-old Jim Wing joined CVS as the pharmacy supervisor for the company's southern Ohio stores. What influenced his decision? "I'm too young to retire. [CVS] is willing to hire older people. They don't look at your age but your experience." Pharmacy technician Jean Penn, age 80, has worked in the business since 1942. She sold her own small pharmacy to CVS five years ago and began working in another CVS store the next day. She was recently given a 50-year pin. ("Turns out they don't make 60-year pins," she says.) By giving Penn credit for time served before she joined the company, CVS once again sent a strong signal about the value attached to experience.

Offer Flexible Work

While older employees won't sign on or stick around if the HR processes and culture aren't welcoming, the substance and arrangement of work are even more important. Companies need to design jobs such that staying on is more attractive than leaving. Many mature workers want to keep working but in a less time-consuming and pressured capacity so that they may pursue other interests. And many baby boomers have a direct and compelling need for flexibility to accommodate multiple commitments, such as caring for children and elderly parents at the same time. Flex work—flexible in both where and when work is performed, as well as flexibility in the traditional career path—can offer many attractions and rewards and appeal to employees' changing needs.

The concept of flexible work is not new, of course, and many companies offer it in some form—job sharing, telecommuting, compressed workweeks, and part-time schedules. But such programs are usually small in scale and, in practice, are often taken up by new mothers and others with consuming family commitments. What's more, the implicit bargain is often that employees who participate will see their careers suffer for it. Companies that have successful flex programs not only make these programs easily accessible to older workers but also structure them so that people who participate don't feel that they're being sidelined or overlooked for promotions—and so that participation leads to a win-win for employer and employee.

Look at ARO Incorporated, a business process outsourcer based in Kansas City, Missouri. Six years ago, its staff turnover was at 25%, which limited its productivity as an operator of contract call centers, back-office and forms processing, outbound customer interaction, and more. Kansas City hosts some 90 call centers, so employees had numerous other options, and the applicant pool was shallow.

Michael Amigoni, the company's chief operating officer, soon found a way to cut costs and improve service by upgrading the company's technology to allow some 100 teleworkers to remain off-site. He then actively recruited baby boomers, who were attracted to the flexibility, to fill these jobs. Employees were not permitted to do the work simultaneously with child care, elder care, or pet care, and company managers visited people's homes to make sure they had an appropriate working environment.

While some younger workers signed on initially, the company found that these employees missed having an office community and largely dropped out.

Meanwhile, ARO gained access to a large pool of mature, experienced employees, who, on the whole, have stayed with the company longer than younger employees have. Turns out, they're also a much better match for the company's customer demographics. "ARO has clients in the insurance and financial services sectors, and a lot of the people we talk to are older," says Amigoni. "It helps that the people making the calls are older, because they are in similar circumstances to customers." For insurance companies, a lot of ARO's work is underwriting, which involves asking questions about health, among other things. It's useful to have workers who are facing some of the same health concerns—their own or perhaps their parents'—that their customers are. ARO has found that younger, entry-level workers cannot make these connections as easily. Turnover is now down to 7%, and productivity is up 15%, partly because the company now has more seasoned staff. To boot, the company was able to expand without having to move into a larger facility, which it didn't want to pay for.

Other companies offer flexibility in work assignments to reignite older employees who have come to find their jobs a bit stale—an approach that can be of particular value in appealing to highly paid managerial talent. For example, four years ago, Deloitte Consulting looked at the firm's demographics and realized that by 2003, 40% of its then 850 partners would be 50 or older and eligible to retire at 55. The firm didn't want to lose this talented group of men and women en masse, so it created what it called a Senior Leaders program, which enabled partners in their early fifties to redesign their career paths. (The program, along with a similar program at Deloitte's sister company, Deloitte & Touche, is currently on hold as the two companies reintegrate operations following last year's decision not to separate as planned.)

Here's how the Senior Leaders program worked: Each year, a ten-member global selection committee assessed candidates who had made a unique contribution to the firm and would continue to add significant value. The committee then sat down with each nominated employee to customize a second career with the firm, including flexible hours and work location, special projects, and the opportunity to engage in mentoring, research, training and development, company promotions, or global expansion. Deloitte still has about a dozen active senior leaders, most of whom opted for full-time work in their rejuvenated roles. The partner who launched the program told us: "The biggest surprise was the prestige the program gained. Being a senior leader became extremely prestigious both to the firm and to the clients."

Still other companies appeal to older workers' desire for flexibility by reducing hours in the years leading up to retirement. The reduced hours are an attractive option because it gives workers opportunities to pursue outside interests. At Varian, a leading provider of radiotherapy systems, employees age 55 and over who have a minimum of five years of service and who plan to retire within three years can negotiate a reduced work schedule. The typical arrangement is four days per week the first year and three days a week thereafter. Half-time is the minimum, and two half-timers can job share. Participants retain full medical and dental benefits and can request a return to full-time work if the new schedule results in economic hardship.

We are strong advocates of flexible work, in all the varieties described here, not only because it's a way to entice older workers to continue working but also because it forms the foundation of a flexible new approach to retirement, one that assumes people can continue to contribute in some way well into their "retirement" years.

Introduce Flexible Retirement

Flexible retirement is flexible work in the extreme—a logical extension of the flexible work models just described, where the work may continue indefinitely.

Retirement, as it's currently understood, is a recent phenomenon. For almost all of history, people worked until they dropped. It was only during the Great Depression that, desperate to make room in the workforce for young workers, governments, unions, and employers institutionalized retirement programs as we know them today, complete with social security and pension plans. When the modern notion of retirement was first articulated near the end of the nineteenth century, the designated retirement age of 65 was longer than the life expectancy at the time. Over the last 50 years, the average retirement age declined steadily; in the United States, Great Britain, and Canada, the average retirement age is currently around 62. Meanwhile, life expectancies have increased, leaving more years for leisure.

But in fact, many people don't want a life of pure leisure; half of today's retirees say they're bored and restless. A recent AARP/Roper Report survey found that 80% of baby boomers plan to work at least part-time during their retirement; just 16% say that they won't work at all. They're looking for different blends—three days a week, for example, or maybe six months a year. Many want or need the income, but that's not the only motivator. People tend to identify strongly with their work, their disciplines, and their careers. Many wish to learn, grow, try new things, and be productive indefinitely, through a combination of commercial, volunteer, and personal pursuits. They enjoy the sense of self-worth that comes with contributing to a business or other institution, and they enjoy the society of their peers. For some people, the workplace is their primary social affiliation.

For all these reasons, the notion of retirement as it is traditionally practiced—a onetime event that permanently divides work life from leisure—no longer makes sense. In its place, companies are starting to design models in which employees can continue to contribute in some fashion, to their own satisfaction and to the company's benefit. Some regulations currently restrict our vision of workers moving seamlessly in and out of flexible work arrangements without ever actually retiring. The IRS prohibits defined benefit plans from making distributions until employment ends or an employee reaches "normal" retirement age. And pension calculations often discourage people even from reducing their hours with a current employer prior to retirement because payouts are often determined by the rate of pay in the last few years of work. (For more on these barriers, see the insert "Why So Inflexible?" at the end of this article.) But a growing number of companies have found ways to call on the skills of retired employees for special purposes.

From the standpoint of the employee, these flex programs offer opportunities to mix work and other pursuits. They also offer personal fulfillment and growth, ongoing financial rewards, and continued enjoyment of the society of colleagues. For employers, the programs provide an elastic pool of staff on demand and an on-call cadre of experienced people who can work part-time as the business needs them. Recruiting and placement costs are close to zero because the business is already in contact with these workers, and training costs are minimal. They know the organization and the organization knows them; they fit in right away and are productive without ramp-up time. And they bring scarce skills and organizational knowledge that can't be matched by contractors unconnected with the organization.

Retirees can also act as leaders on demand. Corporations periodically face waves of executive retirements, and many have done a poor job of maintaining the leadership pipeline. A group of experienced executives who can step in at a moment's notice can both fill gaps and help bring the next generation of leaders up to speed.

Typically, these programs allow an employee to take regular retirement and then, sometimes after a specified break in service (typically six months), return to the employer as an independent contractor, usually for a maximum of 1,000 hours a year. (The IRS imposes the hourly restriction to discourage companies from substituting full-time employees with retirees and thus avoiding expenses such as benefits and FICA. Employees who work more than 1,000 hours per year usually need to be contracted through an agency and make their services available to other employers as well.)

While most such programs today lack sufficient scale to make a difference in a company's overall staffing, serving instead as a safety valve and a source of specific skills and experience, large corporations would do well to bring these programs up to scale as labor markets tighten. An example of a program at a scale proportional to the overall employee population is that of the Aerospace Corporation, which provides R&D and systems-engineering services to the air force. The personnel needs of this California-based company vary from year to year and contract to contract, and its Retiree Casual program helps level the staffing load.

Long-term employees can generally retire with full benefits at age 55 or older. As part of the Retiree Casual program, they can then work on a project-consulting basis for up to 1,000 hours per year at their old base salaries, sometimes less, depending on roles and responsibilities. Eighty percent of retirees sign up, and some start back the day after they retire. About 500 retiree casuals are available at any given time, while 200 are working. They work various patterns—most work two days per week, but some work six months on, six months off (the 1,000-hour limit is approximately the equivalent of half-time). A few (three to four a year) are so indispensable that they have to be dropped from the program and contracted via an agency after they hit the 1,000-hour limit. Most participate into their midsixties, some beyond 80.

The program assures the company a degree of "corporate memory," according to George Paulikas, who retired in 1998 at age 62 as an EVP after spending his entire post-PhD career with the company. He was off only a couple of weeks before being asked back to help on a project and has worked part-time ever since—about one-quarter time last year. "You don't want people with enormous experience to just walk out the door. The Retiree Casual program keeps expertise around and helps transfer it to others. People often remark that we don't have many consultants around here. Actually, we do, but they're called retirees, and they already know the business inside out." Paulikas sticks with the program because it allows him to keep his association with the organization but on his own terms. "This program is a pleasant way to keep associated with a great organization, great people, great work. I get to work less often and with less intensity." And because he's not working full-time, Paulikas has been able to pursue other professional interests; he works as a consultant to the Institute for Defense Analyses and is a member of the National Academy of Sciences Space Studies Board.

Monsanto has a similar program, which it calls the Resource Re-Entry Center. It's open to all employees who leave the company in good standing and want to return to a part-time position, though departing employees have to wait six months after leaving a full-time job. Managers are directed to use retirees for job sharing, for cyclical spikes, and for temporary positions in the case of unplanned leaves. They're told not to attempt a reduction in benefit costs by hiring retirees for long-term work. Participants are eligible for company savings and investment plans as well as spot bonuses (though not the normal bonus structure). Originally, participants were limited to 1,000 hours of work per year to ensure the program wouldn't interfere with pension payouts, but Monsanto recently relaxed the requirement for those people whose pensions wouldn't be affected, such as retirees who had received a lump-sum payout.

Jim Fornango, who retired from Monsanto in 1996 at the age of 53, has returned to work on a variety of projects since 1998. He likes the flexibility: "I spend the amount of time I want doing things I want. I'm not locked into a structure." And, like Paulikas, he's been able to explore other interests at the same time; he serves as a substitute teacher and as a counselor to other teachers.

I T'S FASHIONABLE to invest heavily in high-potential employees, creating programs that give these select (and historically young) people the leadership experiences they'll need to ascend quickly through an organization. Why not, then, develop a similar type of program aimed at older and midcareer workers with the skills, abilities, and experiences that your organization most needs? A lifelong-contributor or high-retention program could call on a variety of techniques to reengage these valuable players. Such a program might include fresh assignments or career switches, mentoring or knowledge-sharing roles, training and development, and sabbaticals—all of which have the potential to rejuvenate careers while engendering fresh accomplishments and renewed loyalty.

And yet in our research, we didn't find a single company that explicitly created such high-retention pools among over-55 workers. Some businesses are taking the first step: Sears, for example, has expanded its talent-management and retention focus to include not just highly promotable people but also solid contributors and pros with specific, tough-to-replace skills. Dow Chemical has oriented its human resource management systems toward "continuous rerecruitment" of its workforce, in part by encouraging people to move into different roles throughout their careers. And companies like Aerospace and Monsanto are using their retiree programs to retain employees with valuable skills. But by and large, in most companies, the over-55 crowd continues to get very little attention from management.

That's going to have to change. Sixty-five isn't what it used to be. In 2001, Bob Lutz, then 69, was recruited to join General Motors as vice chairman of product development, charged with rejuvenating the product line as he had done at Chrysler with the Dodge Viper, Chrysler PT Cruiser, and Dodge Ram truck line. In last fall's World Series, the winning Florida Marlins were led by 72-year-old Jack McKeon, called out of retirement early in the season to turn around the fortunes of a youthful but underperforming club. Collecting Grammy Awards in 2000 were Tony Bennett, Tito Puente, and B.B. King—combined age around 220. Al Hirschfeld's caricatures graced the print media for more than 75 years, and he was still drawing when he passed away last year, his 100th. And then there's the litany of business executives called out of already active retirement to inject stability, direction, confidence, and sometimes legitimacy into major corporations in need of leadership. Examples include 67-year-old Harry Stonecipher, who recently succeeded Phil Condit as Boeing's CEO; John Reed, named interim chairman and CEO of the New York Stock Exchange; Allan Gilmour, vice chairman of Ford, who rejoined the company after retirement; and Joseph Lelyveld, who stepped in temporarily at the *New York Times* last year.

But then, maybe 65 was never what we thought. Lee Iacocca once told *Wired,* "I've always been against automated chronological dates to farm people out. The union would always say, 'Make room for the new blood; there aren't enough jobs to go around.' Well, that's a hell of a policy to have. I had people at Chrysler who were 40 but acted 80, and I had 80-year-olds who could do everything a 40-year-old can. You have to take a different view of age now. People are living longer. Age just gives experience. Besides, it takes you until about 50 to know what the hell is going on in the world."

What Iacocca understood was that people don't suddenly lose the talent and experience gained over a lifetime at the flip of a switch. It's not good business to push people out the door just because your policies say it's time. Smart companies will find ways to persuade mature workers to delay retirement or even eschew it entirely as long as they remain productive and healthy.

Why So Inflexible?

IN AN IDEAL WORLD, flexible retirement would allow employees to move in and out of the workplace seamlessly, without ever choosing a moment to retire. Employers would offer flexible work, compensation, pension and benefits arrangements, subject to sensible and straightforward tests of fairness and merit. Employees would have the option of entering a flexible work arrangement not at some fixed age but whenever it's desirable and feasible, putting together an appropriate combination of salary and "retirement income." Health insurance and other benefits would be portable from employer to employer, and the government would ensure a health-care safety net for all. Employers would need reasonable flexibility in selecting employees and legal protection from discrimination claims from those workers not selected. Flex retirement would embrace a variety of trajectories—different work for a former employer, the same type of work for a new employer, a career restart, variable schedules.

But in the United States, at least, things don't yet work that way, and truly flexible retirement is not yet possible for most employees of publicly held for-profit corporations. Indeed, according to an Employment Policy Foundation study, 65% of employers in the United States would like to offer such flexible retirement, but most feel blocked by regulatory restrictions. The obstacles start with pension and benefits regulations:

IRS. Internal Revenue Code regulations prohibit defined-benefit pension plans from making distributions until employment ends or the employee reaches "normal retirement age." Coupled with an ERISA provision, this can prohibit distributions even after normal retirement age.

ERISA. The Employee Retirement Income Security Act imposes rules of uniformity in the treatment of employees and their pension benefits. These rules make it hard to construct arrangements for the skilled and valuable employees whom companies most want to retain.

ADEA. The Age Discrimination in Employment Act requires equal benefits, such as health insurance, regardless of age. The implications of this law have yet to be sorted out, but it raises the question: Can benefits be reduced as part of a flexible retirement arrangement?

Working around pension regulations can complicate the design of flex retirement programs. The regulations may also impel employees, for financial reasons, to retire altogether (or return altogether) rather than opt for flex retirement. Legislative changes are required to overcome these regulatory impediments, and major employers may have to band together in lobbying for them. The Employment Policy Foundation has outlined the needed changes:

- Amend pension rules to prohibit reductions in pension benefits if an employee's pay is reduced owing to flex retirement.

- Eliminate the 10% penalty on early distribution to employees with 30 or more years of service, regardless of their age, and allow distributions from 401(k) plans before age 59.

- Allow people ages 55 to 65 to buy Medigap insurance at competitive rates.

- Liberalize nondiscrimination tests for flexible retirement plans.

Recent attempts to change these laws have stalled, and the gradual raising of the Social Security full payout age and easing of restrictions on outside income offer relief only for the already retired. The U.S. government has yet to face the demographic and economic imperative to make it easier for mature employees to work.

The costs of health benefits, which have been rising at double-digit rates annually, complicate matters further. Employers are motivated to reduce these costs by reducing coverage for employees and retirees. And because costs and premiums increase with age, employers have a disincentive to retain older workers. As the number of retirees grows, their health benefits become a significant proportion of an employer's fixed costs. In response, more and more employers are taking strong, sometimes draconian, action: Almost everyone is increasing employee premiums and copayments, some are lowering contribution levels and raising eligibility requirements, and a few are eliminating retiree health coverage. Employees are afraid to take advantage of flex retirement programs if it means their health care costs go up.

About the Research

OUR YEARLONG RESEARCH PROJECT, "Demography Is Destiny," concluded in the fall of 2003 and was conducted by the Concours Group in partnership with Ken Dychtwald and Age Wave. Sponsored by 30 major public and private organizations in North America and Europe, the project explored the emerging business challenges presented by workforce aging and other profound shifts in workforce demographics. On the basis of our findings, we developed a series of management actions and pragmatic techniques for anticipating, coping with, and capitalizing on those changes. Member organizations shaped the focus and direction of the project, shared their experiences as part of the field research, and participated in a series of workshops. (For a management summary of our research findings, see http://www.concoursgroup.com/Demography/ DD_MgmtSumm.pdf.)

Originally published in March 2004
Reprint R0403C

About the Contributors

RICHARD W. BEATTY is a professor of human resource management in the School of Management and Labor Relations at Rutgers University in New Brunswick, New Jersey. He is coauthor of *The Workforce Scorecard: Managing Human Capital to Execute Strategy* (Harvard Business School Press, 2005).

BRIAN E. BECKER is a professor of human resources in the School of Management at SUNY Buffalo in New York and coauthor of *The Workforce Scorecard: Managing Human Capital to Execute Strategy* (Harvard Business School Press, 2005).

STEVEN BERGLAS is an executive coach and management consultant who spent twenty-five years as a faculty member in the department of psychiatry at Harvard Medical School. He is the author of four books on how high achievers cope with success, including *Reclaiming the Fire: How Successful People Overcome Burnout* (Random House, 2001).

JEFFREY M. COHN is the president of Bench Strength Advisors in New York, a former research associate at Harvard Business School in Boston, and a former fellow at Yale School of Management's Chief Executive Leadership Institute in New Haven, Connecticut.

JAY A. CONGER is the Henry R. Kravis Research Chair in Leadership Studies at Claremont McKenna College, in California, and a visiting professor of organizational behavior at London Business School. He conducts human resources research with the Center for Effective Organizations at the University of Southern California's Marshall School of Business, in Los Angeles.

KEN DYCHTWALD is the founding president and CEO of Age Wave, a San Francisco-based think tank and consulting firm focused on the maturing marketplace and workforce.

TAMARA J. ERICKSON is the president of the Concours Institute, the research and education arm of the Concours Group, a professional services firm.

LYNDA GRATTON is a professor of management practice at London Business School and author of *Hot Spots: Why Some Teams, Workplaces, and Organizations Buzz with Energy— and Others Don't* (Berrett-Koehler, 2007).

SYLVIA ANN HEWLETT is the founder and president of the Center for Work-Life Policy, a New York-based not-for-profit organization. She also heads up the Gender and Public Policy Program at the School of International and Public Affairs at Columbia University in New York.

MARK A. HUSELID is a professor of human resource management in the School of Management and Labor Relations at Rutgers University in New Brunswick, New Jersey. He is co-author of *The Workforce Scorecard: Managing Human Capital to Execute Strategy* (Harvard Business School Press, 2005).

RAKESH KHURANA is an associate professor of organizational behavior at Harvard Business School and the author of *Searching for a Corporate Savior: The Irrational Quest for Charismatic CEOs*.

CAROLYN BUCK LUCE is the global managing partner for Ernst & Young's health sciences industry practice in New York. She is the cochair for the Center for Work-Life Policy's Hidden Brain Drain task force.

ROBERT MORISON is an executive vice president and the director of research at the Concours Group, an advisory services firm in Kingwood, Texas.

DOUGLAS A. READY is a visiting professor of organizational behavior at London Business School and the founder and president of ICEDR, a global talent management research center in Lexington, Massachusetts.

LAURA REEVES is a senior manager with A.T. Kearney's transformation practice in Atlanta, specializing in organizational effectiveness.

Index